Adults
Only

Adults
Only

I.C. Fingerer

Sheridan Avenue Books

WWW.SheridanAvenue.Com

A Division of Bernard Hanan & Co. Publishers

ISBN 0976809400
Library of Congress Control Number: 2005903475

First Edition

Contents

Dedicated to My Parents,
My Greatest Teachers

Introduction

He couldn't wait to be with her again. He absolutely loved her. Admittedly, he barely knew her. They had met less than twenty hours ago. All he knew about her was her first name and cell phone number. But the previous night spent together . . . .

The entire day he stumbled around in a stupor, anxiously waiting to call her so that they could be together again. He loved her so.

Evening came. He had promised to call at seven. He fumbled with the telephone, awkwardly dialing her cell phone. With his heart pounding and adrenaline pumping, he listened to the repeated ringing of her phone. Finally, a woman answered. She didn't sound like his love. She sounded much older than his love. She sounded sad.

"Melissa?" he asked.

"No," the woman answered, her voice strained. "It's Melissa's mom. Here, I'll let you talk to Melissa."

"Hello," a weak voice sounded in his ear.

"Melissa, baby. It's your love. Remember me from last night? You okay, beautiful?"

A long pause filled him with dread. Had she changed her mind? Did she no longer love him? Finally she spoke. "Do you really love me?" she asked.

"Of course I do!" he insisted. "What kind of question is that? I adore you. I can't live without you."

"Well, then, come visit me," she said diffidently.

"I'm on my way. But, by the way, where do you live? I don't even know what part of the city you live in."

She gave him an address in Staten Island, with a floor number and room number.

Strange, he thought. He had no idea his love was from Staten Island. From the night spent together, he thought his love was high-class. He was surprised at the address she gave him. Not exactly an upscale neighborhood, he thought.

He shook himself. What did he care where she came from? None of that made a difference. He couldn't wait to spend another night with his love. Oh, how he relished the thoughts of being together with his beloved Melissa!

During the entire drive to Staten Island, the only thing that dominated his mind was the enormous love he felt for Melissa.

He exited the highway and made his way to the address. It turned out to be Staten Island University Hospital. At first he felt duped. Had she given him a false address? Was she trying to dump him? Was his soul-enthralled love for her not reciprocated? Then it occurred to him that she was probably a nurse or a nursing student. Either she lived at the hospital, or she was on duty and couldn't wait until after her shift to see him.

He parked the car and raced into the hospital. He was so excited. He would soon be with his love.

The guard stopped him. He explained that he was going to the seventh floor. "That's the burn unit," remarked the guard, "the finest in New York City."

Hmm . . . he was learning more about his love. She wasn't only beautiful, but she was also a nurse or a nursing student in the city's finest burn unit.

He took the elevator to the seventh floor. As he passed the nursing station, a nurse asked him, "Who are you looking for?"

"I'm looking for Melissa," he replied dumbly, embarrassed that he didn't know her last name. "You know, she's got really nice blond hair. She works in room #502."

"Oh, you mean Melissa O'Connell. Yes, she's expecting you."

It was the first time he heard his love's last name. O'Connell. She must be from an Irish family. Interesting, he thought.

"This is the burn unit, so you will have to put on gloves and a gown," said the nurse.

He prepped up.

"Let me take you to Melissa," said the nurse.

He entered room #502. No one was there except a patient, entirely wrapped in bandages, and an older matronly woman sitting beside the bed.

"I'm sorry to intrude," he apologized, "but I'm looking for Melissa O'Connell."

A faint voice from bed replied, "I'm Melissa. It's me, your love. Come closer, my darling. I'll tell you what happened. After I got home in the early morning, I took a nap. My mother was at work. I was alone in the house when it caught fire—an electrical fire. I'm lucky I survived. I was so thrilled when you called. It took all my energy to talk to you. You made me feel so much better when you said I was your love. I'm so happy you came. You must truly love me."

He stared at the mummy-like form before him. Where was her luscious blonde hair? Her gorgeous face? Her sumptuous figure? He was appalled and horrified. This wasn't his love. "I, um, I-I-I," he stammered.

"What's the matter?" she whispered hoarsely. "It's *me* . . . the same girl you said you loved so much last night. It really is *me*. I promise."

"No, no," he finally responded, shaking his head. "I wish you all the best. I hope you recover. But, I have an appointment. Really, I must be leaving." He fled from the room.

In the car on the way home, he thought, "So Melissa really isn't anything so special."

That night he returned to the club looking for a girl he could love.

Do I love you because you are beautiful or are you beautiful because I love you?

—Cinderella

If you care about the person and love them, they become
increasingly beautiful to you, no matter what their objective
rating would be.

—Dr. I. Herschkopf

Is love attraction? Is love desire? Is love lust? Is love selfish?

Dr. Isaac Herschkopf, a psychiatrist on faculty at NYU-Bellevue
Medical Center has a different perspective on love. He explains that
often the very first thing we feel for someone is physical/sexual
attraction. "You never love someone when you first meet them. To say
that you meet someone and you fall in love is an insult to the concept
of love. At most what happens when two people first meet is a feeling
of infatuation."

There is a colossal distinction between *desire* or *attraction* verses
love. Desire or *attraction* may be part of the determinants that enable
babies to come into this world but it is only through *love* that they
endure.

There seems to be no more an important subject than how we, as a
society, define love. The way we define love influences our very lives.

How should we as a society define love? You can attempt to ponder
and theorize a response to this question, but it is axiomatic that your
response will be limited by your own background and education.
Everything is relative.

To accurately understand these concepts, we must seek guidance
from a source that is untainted by trend, time, or geography. You have
heard about living on the edge. I am talking about a different way of
life. It's called living absolute.

✳ *Disclaimer* ✳

According to the law of the United States of America, unless you are 18 years old, it is illegal for you to purchase a book entitled "Adults Only."

You consider this and you remember back to the time when you walked in to a store to buy a beer—you were carded. You were only 17. You were legally underage. You couldn't get the drink. Darn! What a stupid law! In Thailand, Vietnam and China there is no minimum age for drinking. In Switzerland fourteen is the legal age. In France, Italy and Poland one can be sixteen and enjoy a drink. In Canada, Russia, and Mexico the age is eighteen. In Japan and Iceland you have to wait, what seems a lifetime—until you are twenty years old to sample a vodka or beer. In the USA the law is most brutal: one must be twenty-one years of age to legally purchase a drink. In the United States of America you are not considered mature, adult, or responsible until 21 years of age. Even then you are not considered fully developed, as you must wait until 25 to be deemed "adult" enough to rent an automobile.

Yet, most states in America allowed you at a mere 16 years of age, and in some cases even younger, to operate the potentially most fatal and dangerous weapon—a vehicle. Doesn't that take "maturity" and "responsibility"?

You realize that by 16 years old, although you were too young to vote for an elected official, in most states you were legally allowed to have sex. In some cases in Iowa and Missouri, at the tender age of 14 it is legal, while in Colorado you only had to wait until you turned 15.

When you went into an adults only store to purchase some indecent material, again you were carded. You learned that you must be 18 years old in order for such material to be made available to you. Of course you can always find such material online without any restrictions, but that isn't the point. You are infuriated. How does the law reconcile the fact that you are legally of age to get someone else or personally become pregnant (and risk contracting a sexually transmitted disease that afflicts 3 million teenagers a year) but not considered adult enough to see porn?

You arrived at home and signed on to your DSL Internet connection to relax (and download some hot material) only to be interrupted by a phone call. It was the army looking to enlist you. The recruiter gave you a real sales pitch. They will pay for your college, you will get to see the world, and you will even carry a machine gun. You thought this out. You are not adult enough to drink or go into an adults only store but you are adult enough to drive a vehicle, make a baby, and be entrusted with an automatic!

We are dealing with a critical decisive issue: What makes an adult? What makes something "Adults Only"?

No matter your age read this book and find out.

Disrobing

One

Animal House

J ust as I was about to complete my magnum opus, *Adults Only*, I suffered a personal crisis. Justin, my dog, had a severe bout of manic depression. I rushed my beloved canine to the emergency room. The veterinary psychiatrists strapped Justin to intravenous lines and administered mega doses of Prozac. The dog's personal advocate, from the city's Department of Pet Welfare, mandated that I spend the night at the hospital.

At approximately 3:00 AM—just when I was catching a snooze—I received a startling call on my cell phone. My wife, already traumatized by this family tragedy, informed me that Olivia, my darling cat, had suffered mental trauma from observing Justin's ordeal. Olivia needed an immediate treatment of Valium. (It seems that Prozac would have posed an inherent danger for the feline because it is the equivalent of giving a human being LSD.)

The two medications averted a major catastrophe, but both dog and cat needed months of therapy with a noted Park Avenue psychotherapist. Justin's health insurance company refused to issue reimbursement for his daily therapy regimen. My finances were stretched to the limit.

At this critical juncture in my life, tragedy struck. Olivia, my one and only cat (my eyes brim with tears as I write these words), suffered a severe allergic reaction to Valium. The veterinary physicians fought valiantly to save her. We spared no costs. Olivia was rushed to the I.C.U. and attached to a heart-lung machine but, alas, she died. The shock was unbearable.

Nurse Hutchinson at the I.C.U. recommended an efficient and respectable funeral home. The funeral director gave me a choice of caskets and prices. They ranged from pine to mahogany and started at $1,000. A cemetery that provided perpetual care was located and the wake was scheduled. Fortunately, I was able to save the expense of hiring a clergy member to conduct the service. True, in seminary I was never instructed on performing an animal funeral, but I improvised, and all the mourners present considered my eulogy a touching, fitting memorial to a very special cat.

Then something marvelous happened. While waiting in the therapist's waiting room, my dog met Julie, another dog of the opposite sex. It was love at first sight. The romance was palpable. It was a brief courtship, but all were in agreement that Justin and Julie were ready for commitment. Now we had to locate another therapist who specialized in pre-marital counseling. Julie's owner insisted that we appoint a lawyer familiar with veterinary prenuptials. The wedding was arranged. A tailor was hired to custom-tailor a tux and bridal gown for the bride and groom.

Then I received a call from the pet advocate. He complained that the $125,000 state-of-the-art kennel I purchased was not satisfactory for the new couple. The advocate informed me that the chimpanzees employed by the United States Air Force were endowed with a 10.6-million-dollar retirement home in Florida, replete with swimming facilities and a golf course. In light of this, my arrangements for the new couple were substandard and frugal.

As the advocate was drilling sense into my head, I noticed that my precious carnival goldfish was about to ascend to the top of the fishbowl upside-down. Understanding that this signaled that my dear goldfish was in severe cardiac distress, I hung up abruptly with the advocate and called up a renowned goldfish micro-surgeon. He gave me meticulous instructions on how to express-mail the goldfish. He would operate on the fish the next day for a fee of $3,000.

I painstakingly followed the surgeon's instructions. Amidst the bedlam, I was also in the process of sending my manuscript to the publisher. Only later did I realize that I had confused the mailing boxes. The next day, an irate editor called me, declaiming that if my idea of a best-selling book was an almost dead goldfish in a box, then my book contract was cancelled. No sooner did I hang up, stupefied, than the surgeon called to say that he had failed to find the critically ill goldfish among the pages of my *Adults Only* manuscript.

Before I depress you too much with my plight, I must admit that, although I adore animals, I am not a pet owner. All of the elements in the above account did in fact happen, but not to me, and not to a single hapless pet owner. The above parody is a composite of **factual** material contained in *Herd on the Street: Animal Stories from the Wall Street Journal,* by Ken Wells, a *Wall Street Journal* editor.

Pet care in America is no joke. It is a $32,000,000,000 industry. The above satire does not even touch on the latest phenomenon: day care centers for pets so that they can receive proper recreation and learn how to interact with their peers.

One may wonder: Do animals really need to learn etiquette and proper social interaction? What is the point of clothing animals? Is it proper to expend money on luxury accommodations for animals when hundreds of thousands of children are homeless? Is it ethical to spend thousands of dollars to save a carnival goldfish when human beings are dying of disease for lack of basic medical treatment? Should pets be receiving psychotherapy while abused children wait for government allocations before their therapy can commence?

Perhaps I am troubled by these questions because, as a perennial student of world history and sociology, I have noticed that throughout history an *inverse* relationship exists between humans' concern for animals and humans' concern for other human beings. Civilizations and societies that engaged in dressing up the animal tended to dress down the human.

Two examples, one from ancient history and one from modern history, will suffice to illustrate this point. The civilization of ancient

Egypt enslaved human beings at the same time that they literally worshipped animals. Ancient Egypt flourished on slave labor. The pyramids and other grandiose structures were built by slaves—human beings who were cruelly mistreated, forced to work beyond their capacity, and tortured into submission. At the same time, the ancient Egyptians worshipped a whole pantheon of animals: Apis, a bull; Thoth, an ibis; Anubis, a jackal; Sekhmet, a lioness; Sebek, a crocodile; Bast, a cat; Setekh, a hound; Uadjit, a cobra; and Taurt, a hippopotamus.

A similar inversion of values between human and animal reigned in Nazi Germany. Hitler, who murdered millions of human beings, was a vegetarian. As Nazi victims were sent to death camps, "humane societies" were established to take care of their now abandoned pets. Rudolf Hoess, the commandant of Auschwitz, had two pet dogs whom he loved. Visitors to inter-war Berlin witnessed household pets dressed in pants and sweaters.

The most emphatic contemporary effort to obliterate the distinction between human beings and animals comes from Princeton Professor of Bioethics Peter Singer. Prof. Singer, the inaugurator of the animal rights movement, is a champion of "animal liberation," which he equates with the liberation movements of blacks and of women. As he writes[1]:

> I shall suggest that having accepted the principle of equality as a sound moral basis for relations with others of our own species, we are also committed to accepting it as a sound moral basis for relations with those outside our own species—the nonhuman animals.

> . . . This attitude [against such equality] reflects a popular prejudice against taking the interests of animals seriously—a prejudice no better founded than the prejudice of white slave owners against taking the interests of blacks seriously.

Prof. Singer coined the pejorative term "speciesists," akin to "racists" and "sexists," to describe people who "give greater weight to the interests of members of their own species when there is a clash between their interests and the interests of those of other species."

---

[1]   *Practical Ethics* (Cambridge: Cambridge University Press, 1979), chapter three.

Prof. Singer is fond of exclaiming, "We are animals!" He responded to the recent decision of the State of Massachusetts to recognize same-sex marriages by endorsing the next frontier: marriages between humans and "nonhuman animals."

Is it a coincidence that Prof. Singer, whose career started by championing the equality of animals with humans, has in later years become infamous for his enthusiastic support of infanticide and euthanasia? He has written, "Killing a defective infant is not morally equivalent to killing a person. Sometimes it is not wrong at all."

Prof. Singer cannot be dismissed as an eccentric intellectual. His book *Practical Ethics* is one of the most widely used texts in applied ethics, and he is the author of the major article on Ethics in the current edition of the *Encyclopedia Britannica*.

Could Prof. Singer be right? Is there no essential distinction between humans and animals? Instead of my dog Justin marrying his fellow canine Julie, should Julie have married Prof. Singer?

The Soul of the Matter

Is there a distinction between humans and animals, and, if so, what is it?

Physiologically we are more or less the same. Science recently revealed that chimpanzees have a 99.4% genetic similarity with humans. There are even those scientists who are seeking to propose that chimpanzees be classified as *Homo sapiens*.

Even our daily activities are more or less the same as most animals. Both humans and animals eat, sleep, socialize, play, mate, propagate, tend to their young, and live in social groups. Where do we differ from animals?

Prof. Singer, in his attempts to prove that, "the differences between us and the other animals are differences of degree rather than kind," summons—and dismisses—a list of supposed differences:

> It used to be said that only humans used tools. Then it was
> observed that the Galapagos woodpecker used a cactus thorn
> to dig insects out of crevices in trees. Next it was suggested that
> even if other animals used tools, humans are the only tool-making

animals. But Jane Goodall found that chimpanzees in the jungles
of Tanzania chewed up leaves to make a sponge for sopping up
water, and trimmed the leaves off branches to make tools for
catching insects. The use of language was another boundary
line—but now chimpanzees and gorillas have learnt the sign
language of the deaf and dumb, and there is evidence that whales
and dolphins have a complex language of their own.

Perhaps Professor Singer is right. If the singular difference between
animals and humans is based on the mere fact that we physiologically
surpass monkeys by 0.6%, then we are only different in degrees and
not kind. How dare we then discriminate between animals and human
beings?

In fact, in many ways, we are inferior to various animals. We could
in no way compete with the swimming speed of the majority of fish.
Our agility cannot compare to that of the monkey. An elephant can lift
weights with its trunk that the strongest human being would collapse
under. A dog's olfactory sense is 10,000 to 100,000 times stronger
than ours. A blind bat, through its sonar ability, can maneuver its way
through the most complex obstacle course.

Prof. Singer notes, "That there is a huge gulf between humans and
animals was unquestioned for most of the course of Western
civilization." Why? Because most people believed in the Biblical story
of God creating man "in His own image." The Bible states that God
blew into Adam a soul, an immortal soul. This soul formed the essential
distinction between humans and animals.

Significantly, the very same Biblical verse recounts God's plan for
the creation of man and the divine mandate for humans to have
dominion over animals: "God said: 'Let us make man in Our image, in
a form worthy of Us, and they shall exercise dominion over the fish of
the sea and the birds of the sky and over the beasts of the land and over
all creeping things that creep upon the earth.'"

The human being's superiority to animals seems to be only because
of this alleged divine soul.

If I can demonstrate the existence of such a soul, even Peter Singer
would have a reason to eat hamburgers and let handicapped infants live.

Plants, Animals, and Human Beings

Let's say that for some reason you were delegated a job to make a plant happy. How do you make a plant happy? Give it the right amount of light, air, and water, and you'll have a happy plant.

Your next assignment is to make an ox happy. How do you make an ox happy? An ox needs more than a plant. If you gave the ox only light, air, and water, not only would it not be very happy, but you'd have one disgruntled ox. In addition to light, air, and water, the ox needs food, exercise, and the opportunity to propagate. Give an ox a manger full of barley, hitch him to a plow, and don't interfere with his mating season, and you'll have a very happy ox. Oxen supplied with all six of the above ingredients seldom complain of depression.

Now, here comes the challenge: How do you make a human being happy?

We won't even attempt to give the human just light, air, and water. If photosynthesis didn't work to satisfy the ox, it certainly won't work for the human being. How about giving him the same ingredients as the ox—give him food and a job, and make sure he doesn't have sexual deprivation?

Is this a recipe for human happiness? I wonder how many of the 17,000,000 Americans who are diagnosed with clinical depression every year are well nourished, have jobs, and are sexually active. Probably most of them. In fact, the country with the highest rate of suicide in the world is Sweden, a wealthy country with virtually no poverty, full employment, and total sexual freedom.

There is obviously a drastic difference in how to define happiness when it comes to an animal verses a human being. What is the missing link?

Dr. Abraham Maslow spent years studying psychologically healthy people. His research pointed to a "hierarchy of needs" experienced by human beings. On the lowest rung of this ladder are physiological needs such as air, water, food, sleep, sex, etc.—those needs humans share with animals. When those needs are satisfied, however, the human being does not rest contented. Instead s/he feels the need for safety, i.e. stability and consistency. When this need is satisfied, the human being hungers for love and closeness. After achieving love, humans long for esteem. When all these "lower" needs are satisfied, the human being feels the need for self-actualization, which Dr. Maslow defines as "the desire to become more and more what one is, to become everything that one is capable of becoming." This <u>uniquely human</u> need manifests as the search for knowledge, peace, esthetic experiences, self-fulfillment, religious expression, and altruistic activities.

No ox or chimpanzee will ever contemplate a Rembrandt painting, seek to learn something that has no bearing on his own personal existence, or join the Peace Corps. This is a qualitative, not quantitative, difference between humans and animals.

The seat of this uniquely human need for self-actualization is purported to be the human soul. Can the existence of the soul be proven?

Where Dwells the Self?

The Catch-22 here is that "seeing is believing," but because the soul by definition is a spiritual, non-physical entity, it cannot be seen by even the most sophisticated electron microscope. So how can I possibly prove that the soul exists?

Virtually all physicists agree that Black Holes exist, even though no one ever has or ever will see one. The extreme density and strong gravitational field of a Black Hole keeps everything, including electromagnetic radiation, from escaping from it. Therefore, Black Holes are impossible to detect by any instrument whatsoever. Their existence is *inferred* by the behavior of other celestial bodies around them. For example, in 1994, astronomers found that an object of 2.5 billion to 3.5 billion solar masses *must be present* at the center of the galaxy M87. That's a pretty big something to infer.

In the same way, we will look at various phenomena that will strongly suggest the existence of a soul.

First, I would like to pose a few questions:

- Neurologist Robert Collins said, "It's amazing that the body feeds the brain sugar and amino acids, and what comes out is poetry and pirouettes." The same biological ingredients travel to the brains of human beings and animals, yet the outcome is so different. Why?

- Point to yourself. Where did you point? In all probability you pointed to your heart. Is your heart <u>you</u>? Isn't the heart just a mass of muscle? Would there be a more appropriate place to point?
- When you say, "I am feeling happy," which part of you is the "I" who is feeling happy? Is it your cerebrum? Your medulla? Your lungs? Your liver? Who is the "I" that owns the feeling?
- If you were a paraplegic, and you heard that you just won the lottery, you would probably feel elation. Which part of you would feel that elation?

Imagine you are home alone late one night. Outside, it is pitch-black. A storm is brewing. The clock strikes midnight. Suddenly you hear a thump. You turn around and, to your utter horror, you see a strange man in a long white coat, brandishing a butcher's knife. He gags you. He explains to you that he is a scientist engaged in scientific impropriety, and that you have no option but to cooperate, or it will cost you your life. With him are two bags. The small bag looks like it contains some instruments. The other bag is quite large; it looks like it's carrying a body.

The mad scientist puts a metal collar on your neck. He removes surgical instruments from the smaller bag. He then takes out a syringe and fills it with an analgesic drug. The last thing you feel is the needle entering your vein. Then you blank out.

While you are under sedation, the scientist gets to work. His agility and skill is remarkable. After making an incision in your neck, he severs arteries, veins, and nerves. Eventually, he successfully removes your entire head. He then pulls out of the larger bag a limp decapitated body. The scientist then takes your head and sews it on to the second body.

As soon as all the sutures are in place, you feel sensation. You regain vision and stare uncomprehendingly at the scientist. He is exuberant. He claps and dances in euphoria. Then he divulges to you his great achievement. He has just conducted the first-ever head transplant!

He explains that just before coming to your house, he had removed his colleague's head. He brought his colleague's body to your home. He then disconnected your head and put it on this body. Finally, he performed plastic surgery, totally altering your face.

You look down at your new body in utter bewilderment. You don't recognize it at all. Not the torso, not the arms, not the legs. Then the mad scientist holds up a mirror. You don't even recognize your own face. Nothing resembles the real you.

Who is the "real you" trapped inside this foreign body?

While this scenario sounds like bizarre science fiction, it isn't. On November 19, 2003, AOL reported that surgeons would soon be performing face transplants: "Face transplants are technically possible and could arguably be less difficult than reattaching a severed finger, surgeons said, but they called for more research into the risks involved before they are attempted." Dr. John Barker, a plastic surgeon at Louisville University in Kentucky, said his team is ready to perform the world's first face transplant.

Head transplants have already been attempted. On March 14, 1970, Dr. Robert White performed a surgery almost identical to the one I described, except that monkeys, not humans, were used. The surgery, which lasted over twelve hours, was performed in the Brain Research Laboratory of Cleveland's Metropolitan General Hospital.

The late Christopher Reeve of Superman fame stated that he was in a severe depression for a lengthy period following the accident that left him a quadriplegic who could not even breath without a machine. Then his attitude changed. His perspective and outlook became optimistic and happy. He embarked on a mission to help others who suffered from paralysis and neurological challenges. How did things change? Christopher Reeve explained that he realized that, "The real me is not my body. The real me is something far, far greater. Happiness isn't limited to my body. Happiness is the pleasure I derive from my wife and children's smiles. Happiness comes from the real me bringing happiness and faith to others."

At this point, you are probably acknowledging that the "real you" is not the body that you've spent a fortune keeping healthy and trying to preserve as sexually appealing. Even if you didn't have your body or its use—due to a macabre operation or a debilitating accident, you would still be you.

Perhaps "the real you" is centered in your brain? Let's investigate this possibility.

The science of cybernetics has discovered many similarities between computers and the human brain. Since computer technology allows one to program a memory transfer, taking all the information contained in one computer and transferring it to another, imagine that electro-magnetic brain transfers were also possible. Information from the brain of one human being would be electro-magnetically transferred to another person's brain.

Imagine that all your information, your memories, knowledge, etc. were transferred to another person. Would that person now be you?

And, now devoid of your memories and knowledge, would you still be you?

An amnesia patient who cannot recall her own name or any of her past history, experiences, and acquired knowledge still has a sense of self. Is that sense of self tantamount to the biological brain?

Consider identical twins. These two human beings share the exact same DNA; they are genetically identical. If "self" is located in the biological brain, then, assuming that these twins are raised in the same exact environment, they should have identical personalities, ambitions, and predilections. Yet experience reveals that even identical twins are disparate individuals with their own unique personalities. If their brains are the same, how can they be different?

Going a step further, let us analyze a potential human clone. Cloning works by extracting DNA from any cell of a person and then denucleating a donor egg and transplanting the DNA of the person being cloned into the egg. The egg is then transplanted into a woman's uterus. The baby who is born is an *exact* genetic replica of the person cloned. Physically the baby and the human being cloned are identical. They have the exact same brains. Will the clone have a different and distinct sense of self or will s/he be like a well-copied CD?

Philosopher of science Sir Karl Raimund Popper wrote,[2] "I intend to suggest that the brain is owned by the self." That means that the real you is an entity separate from the brain.

The famous neurosurgeon Dr. Wilder Penfield stated that the mind is a basic element in itself, which cannot be accounted for by any neuronal mechanism.[3] Other scientists were so perplexed by the mind (as opposed to the brain) that one scientist referred to it as the "Ghost in the Machine."[4] What these scientists refer to as the "mind," religion would call the "soul."

Dr. Penfield drew his conclusions on the basis of research and observations of patients undergoing brain surgery. He noticed that patients could be aware of what was going on in the operating room and, at the same time, when their brains were stimulated with electrodes, they could have vivid flashbacks of the past. These patients would essentially relive past events as if they were happening right then. Yet they were not confused by these simultaneous occurrences. They could actually say to Dr. Penfield, "You made me do that." There was clearly a "self" that was aware and knew what was happening, and there was a brain, or data bank, which was being activated to elicit events from the past.

Dr. Penfield couldn't find any place in the cerebral cortex where electrode stimulation caused a patient to believe or decide something. The functions of the "self" or the real you cannot be accounted for by any neuronal mechanism. As neuroscientist Professor Sir John Eccles, who won the Nobel Prize in physiology, opines,[5] "It is a mistake to think that the brain does everything and that our conscious experiences are simply a reflection of brain activities." In another words, the real

---

[2]   Popper, K.R. and Eccles, J.C. *The Self and Its Brain* (Springer International, New York, 1985)

[3]   *The Mystery of the Mind: A Critical Study of Consciousness and the Human Brain* (Princeton University Press, Princeton, N.J., 1975)

[4]   Ryle, Gilbert *The Concept of the Mind* (Hutchinson, 1949, London)

[5]   *Mind and Brain: the many faceted problems: selected readings from the proceedings of the International Conference on the Unity of the Sciences* (Paragon House, Washington, 1982)

you is more than the biological, neuronal, and chemical systems allowing you to read this book.

The real you must be something that transcends the physical.

As Professor John Eccles wrote:

> I believe that there is an essential mystery in my personal existence, which transcends the biological explanation of the evolution of my body and my mind. It is evident that this belief coincides with the religious concept of the "soul," and its creation by God.

Two

Love When Least
Expected

Late one night in Auschwitz, a starved and emaciated Hasidic man was rummaging through the garbage, desperately seeking a bit of food. Suddenly he heard a noise. He ducked for cover, fearing that an SS guard had spotted him. Instead, a skeletal Jewish teenager emerged from the dark. He had also come to the garbage dump to scavenge for food. The Hasid emerged from his hiding place and beckoned to the boy. He told him that he wished he could offer him some food, but all his scavenging had yielded nothing. He could offer him something else, however. He told the lad that God loves him and that he also loves him. Then he embraced the boy.

Both the Hasid and the boy survived the Holocaust; they remained in periodic contact. When, many years later, the Hasid died, the boy, by now a middle-aged man, came to the family in mourning and told them the story of their father's hug. He claimed that their father's hug had saved his life. It had made him feel human again. Their father's hug had given him faith, fortitude, and the will to survive.

How can a hug save a life? If human existence is limited to the physical dimension, how can something as ineffable as love stave off death?

Joseph Greenstein was a sickly child who was told by physicians that he would not survive past adolescence. Devastated by the news, he ran away from home and joined the circus as a water boy. There he became acquainted with the circus strongman. The circus strongman took the diminutive Joseph under his wing and taught him that strength is not just a matter of developed muscles; rather, strength is the product of will power, stamina, resoluteness, and the power of the mind. Eventually, little Joseph grew up to become the legendary circus strong man, the "Mighty Atom." Although only 5' 4", he was able to perform what the circus billed as "superhuman feats." And he lived well into his eighties.

How can strength of mind counteract the weakness of the body? Which is the real determinant in human life—physical reality or spiritual reality?

Each of the following cases exemplifies the power of the spirit to forge beyond physical limitations:

- Helen Keller, blind and deaf from infancy, broke through her silent, dark world at the age of seven. She learned to read and write using the Braille system. She graduated with honors from Radcliffe College, served on the Massachusetts Commission for the Blind, and traveled and lectured around the world. She authored seven books, one of them a vivid description of her rich spiritual life.

- Aimee Mullins was born without the bones that connect the knees to the ankle; her legs were amputated below the knee on her first birthday. She learned to ski, and also set records for the 100-meter race, 200-meter race, and long jump at the 1996 Paralympics.

- Mikey Butler was afflicted with Cystic Fibrosis. When he was a baby, the doctors told his parents that he wouldn't survive a month. Against all odds, Mikey not only lived 24 years, but also went to college (carrying his oxygen tank from class to class), played drums at concerts for disadvantaged and developmentally disabled children, and became an inspiration to other patients.

All the above examples suggest that invisible, non-physical factors can profoundly affect corporeal reality.

The relationship between mind (i.e. spirit) and body is an emerging field of scientific investigation. Although the soul cannot be measured, its effect on the physical body is manifest in many groundbreaking experiments.

An edition of *The New England Journal of Medicine*[6] published a landmark study demonstrating that a patient's thoughts and expectations can be as effective in healing the pain of osteoarthritis as surgery. In the experiment, one group of patients suffering from osteoarthritis underwent standard arthroscopy of the knee. The other group of patients underwent sham arthroscopy. They were brought into the operating room, had their knee prepped with antiseptic, were given local anesthesia, and were surrounded by sterile drapes. The surgeon requested all the instruments normally used in the true procedure, and he manipulated the knee as if arthroscopy were being performed. The surgeon and his staff imitated the entire surgery as well as post-operative care and follow up procedures, although in fact no surgery was performed. The results showed that the sham surgery worked just as well as real surgery!

Another study involved Parkinson's disease. One of the most debilitating aspects of Parkinson's is the progressive loss of voluntary muscle function. Parkinson's comes about because of degeneration of brain cells that produce dopamine. Boosting the level of dopamine with certain drugs can significantly improve the symptoms. In this experiment, neurologists used PET, a brain scan, to assess dopamine activity within the diseased parts of the brain. One group of Parkinson's patients was injected with a drug proven to boost dopamine levels, while the other group was injected with a placebo. The changes in brain activity were reflected as changes in color on the computer screen. Prior to any treatment the diseased areas of the brain appeared as a pastel blue on the computer screen. The drug that releases dopamine caused these circuits to light up as a glowing orange. With the patients who believed and expected that they were receiving the drug but were instead given a placebo, the PET scan revealed the same intensity and type of color change. In other words, the placebo—or rather the patients'

---

[6]   J.B. Moseley Et al...*A Controlled Trial of Arthroscopic Surgery for Osteoarthritis of the Knee*, The New England Journal of Medicine 347 (2002): 81-88.

expectations—caused the brain to release as much dopamine as the active drug![7]

Another area of non-physical causality now being tested by scientists is prayer. Two major double-blind studies have found a relationship between improved medical outcomes and being prayed for, although this is inexplicable if the spiritual plane of reality is not taken into account.

Two Duke University researchers presented their findings at a meeting of the American Heart Association. In their study of 150 patients suffering from acute heart disease, patients who were prayed for did significantly better than those who were not prayed for, even when the patient was completely unaware of the prayers on his behalf.

And a Columbia University medical school study of women undergoing in vitro fertilization found that the pregnancy rate for women being prayed for was twice as high as for women who were not (50% versus 26%). Neither the women undergoing treatment nor the medical staff caring for them knew of the study. Dr. Rogerio Lobo, Chairman of the Department of Obstetrics and Gynecology at Columbia and lead author of the study, confessed to being completely perplexed by the result.

That thoughts, hopes, expectations, and prayers can produce such demonstrable physical effects reveals the power of the spirit.

The Human U-Turn

In their book *Psychology*, Drs. Carole Wade and Carol Travis write that we humans think of ourselves as the smartest species around because of our astounding ability to adapt to change, come up with novel solutions to problems, invent endless new gizmos, and use language to create everything from puns to poetry. Yet in their own distinct ways, animals are capable of similar feats. The authors write that we can, however, boast of one crowning achievement: "We are the only species that tries to understand its own misunderstandings."[8]

---

[7]   A.J. Stoessl Et al.. *Expectation and Dopamine Release: Mechanism of the Placebo Effect in Parkinson's Disease*, Science 293 (2001) 1164-1166

[8]   *Psychology*, Sixth Edition, Prentice Hall (New Jersey, 2000)

In other words, only human beings are capable of revisiting egregious behavior and implementing correction and change. Only the human soul has the faculty to choose between right and wrong. While animals can change—tadpoles becoming frogs and caterpillars metamorphosing into butterflies—their changes are preprogrammed by instinct. Only a human being can examine his/her life and choose to make an about-face.

Larry Trapp was the Grand Dragon and state leader of the Nebraska Ku Klux Klan. His life was spent spewing forth tirades of racism and anti-Semitism. He hosted a cable television show that propagated his diabolical hatred. He also provided explosives to blow up a Vietnamese church. When he was well into his fifties, affected by the remarkable unconditional love of a local Jewish couple, Larry Trapp repudiated his hate-filled past, quit the KKK, and converted to Judaism.[9]

Animals change in predictable patterns. Only the human soul can engage in self-examination and make unexpected U-turns. Only the human soul is driven to greater and greater accomplishments, to ever-new heights. This dynamic quality is definitive of the spirit. As Dr. Abraham Maslow pointed out [see Chapter One], no sooner does a human being fill a lesser need than s/he aspires to actualize the next level. This is the essential quality of spirit.

Your Spacesuit

The relationship between spirit and body is like a person wearing a garment. At the moment of death, the garment-body is shed and the spirit survives. Yet, as long as the person is alive, the physical body is necessary for the soul to function in the physical world.

This concept can be illustrated by the astronaut in his space suit. The astronaut cannot go up into space "as is." His body could not survive in the atmosphere and environment of space. His intricately engineered spacesuit is absolutely indispensable for his survival in outer space.

---

[9]   *Not by the Sword: How a Cantor and His Family Transformed a Klansman*, Northeastern University Press (Boston 2001).

Imagine that an alien passing by in his spaceship happened to see Neil Armstrong walking on the lunar surface. He would surmise, of course, that the space suit is this two-legged creature. From the distance of his spaceship, the alien has no inkling that the astronaut is actually the entity living inside the space suit.

Let's return to planet earth. In the physical world, your body is your space suit. The "real you" is the soul inside the body.

Another analogy: Imagine that our alien decides to land on planet Earth, let's say in Massachusetts, toward the end of winter. It's difficult to find a suitable landing site because almost all the land is occupied by towns, roads, and forests. Suddenly he spots a secluded, spacious, unoccupied area covered with ice, the perfect landing site. He lands, sets up his equipment to measure the atmosphere on earth, and goes off to explore. A month later he returns, but there's no trace of his spaceship or equipment. Instead, there's a large lake full of migrating birds. How could our hapless alien have known that he had landed on a frozen lake that was destined to thaw at winter's end?

What is the ideal way for the soul to treat the body? On the one hand, a person who devotes his/her life to gratifying and indulging the body is building a home on ice. Just as the ice is certain to thaw, the body is certain to "disintegrate" at the end of life. On the other hand, a person who mistreats and deprives his/her body is cutting a hole in his/her spacesuit. Both approaches are recipes for disaster.

Dr. Judith Mishell, a psychologist who taught at Rutgers University Medical School, suggests the optimum body/soul relationship:

> Picture the body as a horse and the soul as the rider. The main question is who is leading this tandem? Ideally the soul (the "rider") should be the one that leads, counsels and makes choices; the body (the "horse") should be the one that follows. When you know you are the rider, you love your horse and take very good care of it, but you do not let it lead. Picture a horse and rider, climbing up a mountain. They climb higher and higher. There's grass and water, and they eat and drink what they need. The horse gets tired and raises its head. The rider pats the horse and gives it a sugar cube to calm it down. "A little more, a little more," he

coaxes. The rider considers the horse's needs and desires and limits, but the rider sets the pace and determines the goal. The rider is in control.

Letting physical desire dominate life is like letting the horse be in control and lead the rider. We may stumble into a lot of unexpected trouble en route to a green pasture; worse yet, we will miss out on the most glorious aspects of being human. We will never know the deep joy and serenity that come from commitment to the higher goals set by our souls. Our yearning for immortality, our capacity for nobility, our ability to love selflessly and give generously, our ability to sacrifice our individual desires for a higher good, these are some of the goals of the soul. They are not sublimations of basic human impulses and they are not merely acts of self-preservation clothed in noble garb. The powers of the soul are from above not below.[10]

---

[10] *Beyond Your Ego,* (CIS Publishers, New Jersey, 1991)

Three

Adults Only

I had just boarded the airplane on my way to Miami when I noticed a harried, worried-looking, elderly man. Fear of flying was written all over his face. He approached the stewardess and explained that it was his first time flying. The stewardess smiled, spoke to him reassuringly, and sat him in the aisle seat right next to me.

"I want to sit by the window," the man insisted.

"But this is much more convenient, sir," the stewardess pointed out.

"But when I'm nervous I get all hot and sweaty," the man protested. "I'd like to be able to cool off by the window."

The stewardess gently explained that the windows on an airplane are sealed, and that he'd have to manage without fresh air for the duration of the flight. The fellow grew visibly more panicky.

I tried to imagine what urgent business, what looming personal emergency, had compelled this man to board a plane for the first time in his life. Flashing him a friendly smile, I asked, "I see how nervous flying makes you. You must have something very urgent to do in Miami."

His answer astounded me. "I'm going to Miami to vacation for the winter, as I have every winter since I retired six years ago. Every year

I traveled by train, but this year I decided that if I allow my fear of flying to dictate my life, then it isn't my life. It's the fear's life, and I become its puppet, subservient to it. But I won't allow that to happen. I am in charge! It's like I'm pushing the stroller and the fear is the baby inside. I guide the fear to the best of my ability."

Just a few minutes before, I had been feeling sorry for this somewhat pathetic elderly man. Now I was in awe of him! He was taking control of his life, his emotions, his phobias—and all this at an age when it would have been so easy to shrug and say, "This is how I am; there's nothing I can do about it."

Like animals, we humans are pushed by our fears and pulled by our desires. Unlike animals, however, we have the unique human faculty of being able to manage our aversions and cravings. This is what really defines us as "adults."

As the renowned mystic Moshe Haim Luzzatto wrote[11]:

> At the beginning of creation nothing stood against the will of God. Heaven and earth, from the mightiest galaxies to the smallest microbe, reflected only His will. They existed as testimony to the revelation of His Oneness. But this sublime era ceased with the creation of man. Only man has free will. Only he can accept powers other than the Divine. Only he can disobey God's will.

The unique human faculty to choose a course of action that is difficult and distasteful to us, or to refrain from a course of action that calls to us like a siren, is called "free choice." Only a human being can decide to conquer a fear by facing it head-on. Only a human being can decide to return a wallet full of cash that s/he finds on the street—even if s/he doesn't have enough money to pay the mortgage that month.

Free choice operates only in the realm of morality. This means that those who claim that your choices are determined by heredity and environment are right when it comes to choices such as what you'll wear today, which movie you'll pick to see, which car you'll buy, or

---

[11]   In *The Way of God* (Phillip Feldheim, New York, 1999). Translation rendered in *The Wisdom of the Hebrew Alphabet* (Mesorah Publications, New York, 1997)

which profession you'll choose. Only in the realm of moral choice are you truly free.

Free choice is costly. It kicks in only at the point (unique for every individual) where the scales are evenly weighted between both possibilities, and choosing between them is an inner struggle.

In the above example, for instance, let's say Elaine finds a wallet on the street containing $2,000—just the amount she was short in order to pay her mortgage that month. Depending on Elaine's upbringing, it could be totally natural for her to pocket the money without a second thought. No free choice there. Or, it could be totally natural for her to return the money to its owner; she would never consider doing otherwise. No free choice there either. But let's say that, although Elaine was reared to always act honestly, right now she is under great pressure to pay her mortgage so the bank won't foreclose and she just lost her job, so she doesn't see any other way of coming up with the required sum. She picks up the wallet, takes it into her car, opens it, counts the money, and sits there struggling to decide what to do. That's free choice!

Heredity and environment determine the scope of our free choice. On the continuum between good and evil, the infinite possibilities above and below any individual's choice box are closed to that individual at his/her current point of development. For example, for Joe, brought up in a slum where gang warfare is rampant, the possibility of choosing to join the Peace Corps and devote his life to helping third world peasants may not be within his realm of choice. Rather, his free choice is operational when he approaches an all-night gas station and has to decide whether to kill the attendant in order to steal the cash box. If he chooses against killing, he has registered a great moral victory—given the parameters of his choice box. Jennifer, on the other hand, brought up in a solid middle-class family of scrupulous honesty, may never even be tempted to rob a gas station, even when she is seriously short of funds, but she may have free choice whether to make a small omission on her income tax return. If she chooses to cheat, she has registered a great moral failure—given the parameters of her choice box.

In the fall of 2004, researchers at Princeton University corroborated the premise that free choice operates in the realm of morality. They presented the participants of their study with the following moral dilemma: Enemy soldiers have taken over your town and are killing civilians. You and your family are hiding in a cellar. Just as the soldiers enter the house your baby starts to cry. If you don't stifle your baby's crying you will jeopardize every one else, if you stifle the baby it will result in suffocation and the baby will die. What do you do?

Researchers studying the MRIs of the participants of the study marveled at the fact that the MRI showed not only activity in the emotional section of the brain, as would be noticed in a more simplistic decision, but that areas in the brain that focus on abstract reason and cognitive control showed incredible activity. It was clear that the choices that we make that are circumscribed by heredity and environment, don't elicit the type of activity that is found in our truly free choices.[12]

Unfortunately, the neuroscientists that conducted the study denied the unique human aspect of free will; attributing instead the fact that moral choices take longer to make due to evolution. They theorized that abstract reasoning takes place in the more recently evolved parts of the brain. Accordingly, they concluded that a person's moral choices are based on the evolutionary process.

"The Twinkie Defense"

Sadly, the concept of free choice is quite out of vogue these days. Instead, people commit the most heinous crimes and claim that it's not their fault; they had no choice! This attitude complements the scientists' view stated above that moral choices are made in tandem with evolution. If our moral choices are limited to how evolved our brains are then all justifications of deviances are valid.

- "He cut me off in traffic. I had no choice but to pull out my gun and teach him a lesson."
- "She insulted me. I had no choice but to seduce her husband so she wouldn't be one up on me."

---

[12]   Journal *Neuron*, Vol. 44, pp. 389-400. *The neural bases of cognitive conflict and control in moral judgment,* Greene, J.D., Nystrom, L.E., Engell, A.D., Darley, J.M., Cohen, J.D. (2004)

- "My parents were overly strict and repressive. I had no choice but to poison them."
- "It's not my fault that I drowned my young children. My boyfriend had broken up with me, and I was so depressed."

If the above excuses (all of them from real-life incidents) seem ludicrous, consider "The Twinkie Defense." On November 27, 1978, San Francisco City Supervisor Dan White walked into City Hall, pulled out a gun, and, in front of a dozen witnesses, shot to death Mayor George Moscone and fellow City Supervisor Harvey Milk. During the murder trial, White's attorneys claimed that it wasn't his fault. White, you see, is hypoglycemic, and on the way to City Hall, he had stopped at a Seven Eleven and bought a package of Twinkies and a Coca Cola, which he promptly consumed. By the time he reached City Hall, his blood sugar was over the top, so he was no longer responsible for his actions. The Twinkies made him do it!

Incredibly enough, the court accepted this argument and reduced the charge against Dan White from first-degree murder to manslaughter. "The Twinkie Defense" is now the term used in jurisprudence whenever the defendant claims that he should not be held criminally liable for his actions that broke the law, because he was suffering from the effects of allergies, stimulants, sugar, and/or vitamins.

It may seem that humans and scientists gain a lot by denying free will; they can get away with the most outrageous actions and be held culpable of nothing. In fact, humans lose a lot by denying free will. Free will empowers people to change, grow, and mold themselves. Without it, people would be helpless automatons.

I know a man who had a terrible temper. His frequent outbursts made his domestic life hellish. His wife threatened to divorce him and his children were scared of him. One day I met him after a long hiatus, and I asked him how things were going. He told me proudly that he had stopped yelling and had learned to control his temper. I was amazed that a person could change so drastically. I asked him how he did it.

He said: "I was a chain smoker. My doctor told me that if I didn't quit, I'd be dead. So, with a lot of help, I did it! I stopped the habit of a lifetime. Then I said to myself, 'If you can quit smoking, you can do anything.' I decided to conquer my anger problem. That was even harder than quitting smoking, but I worked on myself and did it. My wife and children are so much happier, and you know something? So am I."

A great teacher[13] summarizes this subject as follows: "We are born into the human race and live our lives striving to bring out our humanity. Ironically, one of the greatest quandaries among social thinkers of our times is figuring out what it actually means to be human. Are we cosmic accidents evolved from monkeys or sparks of Godliness formed by the Almighty Himself? Are we separate, solitary entities roving the existential countryside or tiny pieces in some massive cosmic plan? Society's greatest minds have grappled with this and their conclusions range from vague and confused to downright terrifying . . .

The ability to ascend higher than angels and to descend lower than the vilest creature—this is what it means to be human. Built into this potential is the power to persevere, to constantly move upward regardless of the mistakes we might have made. Every day is a new creation, a new opportunity to climb another rung. And climb we must—for that is what being human is all about."

The Global Kindergarten

Some people blame God for creating humans with such a strong propensity to do evil. Perhaps they're right. Imagine how felicitous the world would be if no one felt impelled to kill, steal, abuse, or hurt anyone else. There'd be no terrorists, no murderers, and no unfaithful spouses, and you wouldn't need six locks on your front door plus an alarm system connected to an expensive "armed response" company.

But would life without free choice really be better? Or would it be like a global kindergarten? After all, one of the hallmarks of the maturation process is that with greater maturity, there's greater freedom of choice. A young child is allowed to choose between wearing a red shirt today or wearing a blue shirt, and between chocolate ice cream or vanilla ice cream. A young child cannot be entrusted with significant

---

[13]   R. Shlomo Freifeld (1920-1984), founding dean of the Shor Yoshuv Institute in Lawrence, N.Y.

choices such as where to enroll in school or how often to visit the grandparents. As the child grows, the realm of his choices also grows. Truly free choice is "for adults only."

God demonstrates His faith in humans by giving us free choice. Because we have the ability to choose evil, our decision to choose good is significant and meaningful. In fact, our choices are the only meaningful constituent of our lives. Everything else is provided us, like scenery and stage props. If we had no free will, our lives would be a fatuous exercise of reading a script. Instead, we have the ability to make heroic, ennobling, altruistic, and valiant choices. By so doing, we become true heroes and victors.

Free will is thus the defining characteristic of the true self. As a great scholar put it:[14] "Only one thing, one detail, really constitutes 'me,' and that is the free will given to God by man. Free choice is what constitutes the self, the 'I' in its entirety. Without this choice, the 'self' does not exist."

Just as the seat of hearing is the ears, so the seat of free will is the soul.

The human being has two souls. In addition to the Divine soul that separates the human being from the lower forms of life, man also has an animal soul. The *Zohar* (the authoritative, ancient book on mysticism) explains that man is intrinsically composed of animal and angel. Both animal and *Homo Sapiens* were gifted with a soul that generates life; in metaphysical literature this is called the *nefesh behemis,* the lower soul. Then came a new phase where *Homo Sapiens* became human beings. This was accomplished by the addition of a totally original ingredient— the Divine soul.

Only man can transcend his elemental, animal nature and place himself on a spiritual plane. The spirituality in man may soar to the highest transcendental realm. What defines a human being is the ability to control the physical and animalistic and put it under the direction of the spiritual self.

The ideal relationship between the body (or physical self) and the soul (or spiritual self) is the relationship between a parent and a young

---

[14]   R.Y.M. Tucazinsky quoted in *Beyond Your Ego* (CIS Publishers, 1991)

child. A parent is responsible to take care of his child, providing the child with adequate food, sleep, clothes, etc. A responsible parent doesn't let her child subsist on junk food, sleep five hours a night, and go out in a rainstorm wearing shorts and a t-shirt. Just so, the soul must take proper care of the body, making sure it gets proper food, sleep, etc. A parent is also responsible to provide proper discipline and education. Even so, the soul must discipline the body and educate it in the proper way to behave. When the relationship turns adversarial (e.g. the child has a tantrum because he didn't get the candy he wanted) the skillful parent remains firm, trusting that she knows what is best for the child.

Experienced parents know that children always gravitate toward eating candy, staying up late at night, and amassing all the toys they can get. Such propensities do not cast children as "bad." It is the juvenile nature to choose indulgence and pleasure. Similarly, the body is not "bad" because it gravities toward indulgence and pleasure. But the parent who allows the child to have whatever s/he wants is making a serious mistake. Similarly, the soul that lets the body dominate and domineer is abdicating its responsibility to make wise choices that will ultimately benefit both body and soul.

Atheism
Discombobulated

Four

Panspermia

B
ritish Professor Antony Flew was 21st century's most avowed atheist. He was the most vocal of all modern atheists, proclaiming the lack of evidence for God while teaching at Oxford, Aberdeen, Keele, and Reading universities in Britain, in visits to numerous U.S. and Canadian campuses and in books, articles, lectures and debates. In 1984 he published "The Presumption of Atheism," which played off the presumption of innocence in criminal law. Flew said the debate over God must begin by presuming atheism, putting the burden of proof on those arguing that God exists. His volumes "God and Philosophy" are classics in the field of atheism.

On December 9, 2004 the Associated Press and multiple news wires published the sensational news that the most famous atheist of our time, Professor of Philosophy Antony Flew, renounced his atheism and declared his previous books on the subject obsolete. My first impulse was that this was a premature April Fools Day joke, but it wasn't. At age 81, after decades of insisting belief is a mistake, Dr. Flew the *atheist* became Dr. Flew the *believer*.

We will soon see that it was Dr. Flew's objective scientific research, which caused his transition from atheist to believer.

Intelligent Design

Sir Isaac Newton had a colleague who was a staunch atheist. Newton, who believed in God, would frequently cross words with his colleague on this subject.

One day, the atheist came to visit Newton in his library, and he noticed an extraordinary contraption. Sitting on Newton's desk, reflecting the rays of the afternoon sun, was an exquisite brass engine that depicted the solar system in three dimensions.

"How beautiful!" remarked the atheist.

"You haven't seen anything yet," said Newton. "Do you see the small lever on the base? Move it towards you."

As the atheist moved the lever, the entire object slowly came to life. At its center, the orb of the sun started to revolve. Further out, turning on brass cogs, the planets began their revolutions around the sun, each planet accompanied by its own moons, all moving in breathtaking precision.

"This is amazing!" remarked the atheist, "Who made it?"

"No one" replied Newton, deadpan.

"What do you mean 'No one'?"

"No one. It just sort of . . . fell together, you know."

"No, I don't know! I insist you tell me who is the maker of this priceless object. I refuse to believe that this object merely 'fell together'."

"This," said Newton, pointing to the contraption, "This you insist has to have a maker. But this," Newton said, spreading his arms wide to indicate the entire creation, "This, infinitely more beautiful and complex, you insist has no maker!"

If a simple design, needing only a modicum of basic intelligence and skill, requires more than chance, how much the more so this fantastic world, which is far beyond our intelligence and includes us, too?

As the 2nd century sage Rabbi Akiva summed it up: "As a house implies a builder, a garment a weaver and a door a carpenter, so does the existence of the universe imply a Creator."

It was design that prompted Professor Flew to make, what we called in chapter 2, "the human U-turn." After years of study, he finally concluded that some sort of intelligence or first cause must have created the universe. As Flew says in the new video *Has Science Discovered God*, "Biologists' investigation of DNA has shown, by the almost unbelievable complexity of the arrangements which are needed to produce (life), that intelligence must have been involved."

"Super-intelligence is the only good explanation for the origin of life and the complexity of nature," Flew said in an Associated Press telephone interview from England.

Did the Universe Self-Create?

How intricate is the design manifest in this world? Biologists have discovered that all animals, from cockroaches and crabs to the larger mammals, have an acute sense of time, which resides in an internal biological clock. Diurnal species live by sun time; nocturnal migrants adjust to sidereal (star) time; marine animals live by lunar (tide pattern) time.

The Earth's magnetic field plays a major role in many species' migratory patterns. When baby loggerhead turtles embark on their 8,000-mile trek around the Atlantic, they use invisible magnetic clues to check their bearings. So do salmon and whales, honeybees and homing pigeons, frogs and Zambian mole rats. Scientists theorize that the site of the internal timepiece in the higher sophisticated animals, including birds, must be a complicated nervous organization of several autonomous systems in the brain which, phasing together, amount, in affect, to a cockpit's switchboard, complete with an adjustable sextant (an instrument used to find latitude in sea through altitude of sun) for sun, star, or magnetic compass orientation and a fixed chronometer. What complexity! What order!

Those who maintain that such intricacy is the result of chance mutations and natural selection (i.e. evolution), as Dr. Flew believed for most of his life, must contend with the daunting statistical improbability of their thesis.

There is only 1 in $10^{39,950}$ chance that a single viable bacterium ever evolved on Earth. Remember: This is after we take into

account a billion years' worth of trials. Calculations like
this led Harold P. Klein, chairman of the National Academy
of Sciences Committee on Origin-of-Life Research, to
comment, "The simplest bacteria is so complicated from the
point of view of a chemist that it is almost impossible to
imagine how it happened."

In 1981, Nobel Laureate Hoyle and his associate Wickramasinghe
calculated that these odds constituted "[such] an outrageously
small probability that [it] could not be faced even if the whole
universe consisted of organic soup." Hoyle added that it was
more likely that "a tornado sweeping through a junkyard might
assemble a Boeing 747 from the materials therein."[15]

Nobel Prize-winning chemist-physicist Ilya Prigogine is even more
emphatic. He says, "The statistical probability that organic structures
and the most precisely harmonized reactions that typify living organisms
could have been generated by accident is zero!"[16]

Swiss biochemist Charles Eugene Guye proved through probability
calculus that the formation of even one molecule of living matter by
mere chance is as good as impossible.[17]

In 1953, Stanley Miller and Harold Urey used laboratory conditions
comparable to those of primordial earth to create life. Their model was
made up of the building blocks of the atmosphere, H_2O, H_2, CH_4, and
NH_3. After one week, the team analyzed the contents of the solution
and found a variety of organic compounds, including some of the amino
acids that make up the proteins of organisms. This was considered a
monumental "proof" of the theory of evolution. Scientists thought that
they had created life! Fifty years since the original experiment, however,
scientists still have not been able to create the elements that went into
making the experiment work.

---

[15]   Lawrence Kelemen, *Permission to Believe* (Targum Press, 1990) p. 60.

[16]   *Physics Today,* Volume 25, pages 23-28

[17]   Guye, Charls-Eugene, L'Evolution Physico-Chimique, Lausanne 1947,
        pp.205-240

Evolution

Let us move on to Evolution. The Theory of Evolution is based on several assumptions. We will scientifically examine these postulates to decide whether the theory of evolution is truly based on science or rather grounded in ideological dogma.

1) Evolution assumes that life evolved ever-so-slowly, a step at a time, each new species evolving from another. Is this true?

The only way to answer this question is to research when and where the greatest repository of ancient fossils was found and what we learn from them. In 1909, the director of the Smithsonian Institute, a scientist, Charles D. Walcott, found the world's most important fossils in the Canadian Rockies. It is called The Burgess Shale and it is the best-known, best-described source for a glimpse at the beginning of the evolution of all present-day animals. These fossils originate from the Cambrian Period (according to science, 500 million years ago) when Earth was dominated by water. The atmosphere was thin, and life had yet to crawl out of the sea. How these fossils survived eons of geological time is a remarkable journey in itself.

Most Cambrian evidence was crushed and destroyed by the transition of Earth changing from mostly water to land masses. But a cocoon of hard rock known as the Cathedral Escarpment protected the Burgess Shale. According to science, a few hundred million years later, the mud had hardened into shale and had been lifted from the ocean bottom to an elevation of nearly 8,000 feet. The fossils are extraordinarily well preserved—not just the hard shells that molded most fossils, but also the soft parts of the anatomy. And instead of being flattened, the creatures were deposited in every imaginable position—tilted this way and that.

And there they sat until 1909 when paleontologist Charles Walcott found the Cambrian fossils that he was looking for. Every summer he returned to the Rockies to collect more fossils. Over those years, the treasure trove grew to 30,000 slabs containing 65,000 fossils of some 170 species of Cambrian life.

What is astounding about all this is that all these species were simultaneously present. There was no evolution! This really posed a problem to evolution because these fossils contained representatives from every phylum except just one of the phyla that exist today. No new phyla ever evolved after the Cambrian explosion.

What did Walcott do with his earth-shattering discovery?

Walcott knew that he had discovered something very important. He suffered from what we would today call cognitive dissonance and refused to believe that evolution could have occurred "simultaneously." This was totally against the Darwinian theory that he and his colleagues were indoctrinated with. He chose not to rock the boat of the evolutionists. Walcott reburied the fossils, all 65,000 of them, this time in the drawers of his laboratory in the Smithsonian Institute in Washington D.C. It was not until 1985 that they were rediscovered (in the drawers of the Smithsonian).

In 1989 Harvard Paleontologist and author Stephen Jay Gould wrote a best-selling book called "Wonderful Life: The Burgess Shale and the Nature of History." Gould argued that the presence of 170 widely varied species in the same Cambrian deposit forces a fundamental change in understanding evolution.

The Burgess Shale suggests that scientists were wrong to believe that life evolved ever-so-slowly, a step at a time, each new species evolving from another. From the Cambrian fossils it was patently clear that these diverse species emerged and evolved simultaneously, as Gould said—"a chaotic explosion of life."

Dr. David M. Raup, former curator and dean of Chicago's Field Museum of Natural History, who Stephen Jay Gould once called "the world's most brilliant paleontologist", wrote:

> Instead of finding the gradual unfolding of life, what geologists
> in Darwin's time and geologists of the present day actually find
> is a highly uneven or jerky record; that is, species appear in the
> sequence very suddenly, show little or no change during their
> existence in the record, then abruptly go out of the record [18]. . .

---

[18]   *Conflicts Between Darwin and Paleontology,* an article in *Bulletin* (Field
       Museum of Natural History) # 50 (January 1979)

2) The principle message of evolution is that all life descended with modification from a single primitive source. This source is assumed to be so simple that it could have arisen by chance from nonliving material. Is this true?

Not only is there no scientific justification for this theory but also its repercussions can be outright dangerous. To assume that life arose spontaneously and that the alleged first organism could reproduce itself means that we humans have no intrinsic value. We are the products of chance; essentially we are accidents of nature. Contrast this with the Biblical approach that because man is created in God's image, he is obligated to honor his fellow man and shower him with kindness for by doing so he is honoring God. It follows that he must be careful not to embarrass or abuse another person, for by so doing he is slighting God. This leaves me a bit biased in the battle of Evolutionism vs. Creationism. Yet I will be as objective as possible in determining whether evolution is a tenable theory.

For starters, Macroevolution is scientifically flawed. In order for evolution to work, long sequences of "beneficial" mutations must be possible, each building on the previous one and conferring a selective advantage on the organism. The process must be able to lead not only from one species to another, but to the entire advance of life from a simple beginning to the full complexity of life today. There must be a long series of possible mutations, each of which conferring a selective advantage on the organism so that natural selection can make it take over the population. No one has ever shown this to be possible.

Macroevolution is built upon the false premise that there were evolutionary transitions. The absence of any transitional forms proves that there never were any. Professor N. Heribert-Nillson of Lund University in Sweden spent forty years researching this subject. He summed up his conclusions in his book, *Synthetische Artbildung*:[19] "It is not even possible to make a caricature of evolution out of palaeobiological facts. The fossil material is now so complete that the

---

[19] As quoted in *The Neck of the Giraffe: Where Darwin Went Wrong* (Pan Books, London, 1982), p. 22

lack of transitional series cannot be explained by the scarcity of material. The deficiencies are real, they will never be filled."

The neo-Darwin theory of evolution is based on the type of random mutations that one MIT trained bio-physicist and leading scientist referring to such randomness said, "It is less than the probability of your winning the New York State Lottery seven weeks in a row. Most people would consider such an event impossible."[20]

Macroevolution is based on theory and theory alone.[21] A leading evolutionist admitted the infeasibility of random mutation when he said: "I agree that there are no definitive examples where a macroevolutionary change (such as the development of cetaceans from terrestrial mammals) has been shown to result from a specific chain of mutations. And I agree with your further comment that we have no way of observing a long series of mutations. . . . An equally reasonable conclusion, in my view, would be that our inability to observe such series cannot be used as a justification for the assumption that such a series of mutations did NOT occur."[22]

In a letter to the August-September 2004 issue of Britain's *Philosophy Now* magazine, several months prior to his grand metamorphosis, Professor Flew wrote, "It has become inordinately difficult even to begin to think about constructing a naturalistic theory of the evolution of that first reproducing organism."

3) For years, evolutionists have propagated their theory basing it on the presence of vestigial organs in human and animal bodies.

---

[20]   Dr. Lee Spetner on www.trueorigin.org

[21]   The fossil record; genetic code; speed and effects of mutations; phenomena of biogenesis; and biochemistry—all contradict the theory of evolution. I would recommend the books *Not by Chance: Shattering the Modern Theory of Evolution* (Judaica Press, New York, 1997) by biophysicist Professor Lee Spetner; *Evolution: A theory in Crisis* (Burnett Books, London, 1985) by molecular biologist, Dr. Michael Denton; *Darwin's Black Box: A Biochemical Challenge to Evolution*, by Michael J. Behe (Free Press, 1996); and *Permission to Believe* (Targum Press, 1990) by Lawrence Keleman

[22]   Based on an exchange between Drs. Lee Spetner and Edward E. Max on www.trueorigin.org

Almost all of these proofs have been rebuffed. Biologists who were certain that the thyroid gland and spleen were vestigial ended up humiliated by their errors. As one honest scientist confessed, "Every scientist tries to find something superfluous or redundant in a living creature and always, even the most trivial, has ultimately been found to have its use."[23]

Science is constantly discovering that every item in nature serves a unique function. For example, Michael Zasloff recently discovered that African clawed frogs secrete antibiotics. Cancer-fighting molecules have been obtained from snake venom and the liver of the dogfish shark. Anti-stroke treatments have been derived from the bat and, as is well known, aspirin comes from the bark of the willow tree.

This is not to say that evolution is inherently, patently wrong. There is nothing unscientific or sacrilegious in the evolutionary concept of the origin and growth of forms of existence from the simple to the complex, and from the lowest to the highest. The Bible itself gives an account of gradual ascent from amorphous chaos to order, from inorganic to organic, from lifeless to vegetables, animal and man; insisting however, in the most certain of terms that each stage is no product of chance but is an act of Divine will.

A verse in Psalms proclaims that God fashioned "high mountains for the mountain goats." The commentators explain that at first glance the remote and barren mountains appear to serve no purpose; but in fact they were created to provide a habitat for the wild mountain goats. The writer of the most contemporary translation/commentary of Psalms writes:

> This runs counter to the secular theory of evolution, which teaches that organisms adapt to the specific nature of their particular environments. The Bible teaches, however, that the environment was created to suit the needs of the specific animals, which were destined to live there. Evolution teaches that the high forms of life developed from lower forms, which preceded them, but the Bible teaches that the lower forms of life or nature

---

[23] Anthony Tucker, Cybernetic Insight, Guardian, 3/8/1965

were created to serve the higher forms, which were ordained to follow them.[24]

"Philosophical Necessity"

For centuries and centuries science assumed the eternal existence of the world. This was in direct contrast to the Bible, which described the beginning of the world as an act of creation *ex nihlio*. Religious people who believed that the universe had a beginning were deemed parochial and unscientific. In 1965 a revolutionary discovery cast doubt on the concept of an eternal universe. Penzias and Wilson, two scientists from Bell Laboratories, constructed a massive antenna in their effort to research radio waves. They came up with an incessant amount of interference that they originally attributed to bird excrement. Upon further research, the two scientists discovered that the disturbing interference was none other than the echo of the original sound that emanated from the beginning of the universe, the echo of what has become known as the "Big Bang."

As Dr. Gerald Schroeder, former professor of nuclear physics at M.I.T. wrote:

> The world paradigm changed from a universe that was eternal to a universe that had a beginning. Science had made an enormous paradigm change in its understanding of the world. Understand the impact. Science said that our universe had a beginning— that the first word of the Bible is correct. I can't overestimate the import of that scientific "discovery." Evolution, cave men, these are all trivial problems compared to the fact that we now understand that we had a beginning.

Although it was ridiculed and mocked for millennia, the first word of the Bible became scientifically sound. Incidentally, for this discovery the two scientist were awarded the Nobel Prize.

At the 1990 meeting of the American Astronomical Society, the meeting's chairman, Dr. Geoffrey Burbidge, astrophysicist at the

---

[24]   R. A.C. Feuer in *Psalms* (Mesorah Publications, New York, 1991) p. 1260

University of California at San Diego Center for Astrophysics and Space Science and former director of the Kitt Peak National Observatory commented: "It seems clear that the audience is in favor of the book of Genesis—at least the first verse or so, which seems to have been confirmed."[25]

Dr. Robert Jastrow director of NASA's Goddard Institute for Space Studies wrote of the unprecedented theological implication of this discovery:

> This is an exceedingly strange development, unexpected by all but theologians. They have always accepted the word of the Bible: In the beginning God created heaven and earth... For the scientist who has lived by his faith in the power of reason, the story ends like a bad dream. He has scaled the mountains of ignorance; he is able to conquer the highest peak; as he pulls himself over the final rock, he is greeted by a band of theologians who have been sitting there for centuries.[26]

A renowned physicist and colleague of Penzias and Wilson, asked one of the two scientists after their amazing discovery, "How do you assume the universe came into existence?" The scientist refused to give any thought to the matter. He seemed to opt to never know the answer, rather than consider a Super-Creator.

My physicist friend was troubled by the obstinacy and lack of intellectual openness on the part of the Nobel Prize winning scientist. Aren't scientists dedicated to finding the truth, wherever it may lie? Why should such an eminent scientist reject out of hand—without any objective investigation—the possibility that the world was created by God?

"Then, I realized why," the physicist told me. "Recognition and cognition of a Super Creator—God means the acknowledgment of heavy personal responsibility. This is something the scientific community is not ready for."

---

[25] *Satellite's New Data Smoothly Supports Big Bang Theory*, David Chandler in *Boston Sunday Globe*, January 14, 1990

[26] New York Times Magazine, June 25, 1978

As Robert Jastrow, director of NASA's Goddard Institute for Space Studies, wrote, thirteen years after the major discovery:[27]

> I think that part of the answer is that scientists cannot bear the thought of a natural phenomenon that cannot be explained, even with unlimited time and money. There is a kind of religion in science. . . . This religious faith of the scientist is violated by the discovery that the world had a beginning under the conditions in which the known laws of physics are not valid, and as a product of forces or circumstances we cannot discover. When that happens, the scientist has lost control. If he really examined the implications, he would be traumatized. As usual, when faced with trauma, the mind reacts by ignoring the implications . . .

To quote another scientist: "All that prevents many scientists from accepting Creation as the only possible explanation of nature is a strong dogmatism nurtured by the fear of inescapable logical consequences and moral obligation."[28]

A year after the major event of the Big Bang revelation, Aldous Huxley, scientist, philosopher, and staunch Darwinist, displayed disarming honesty when he said:[29]

> I had reasons not to want the world to have meaning, and as a result I assumed the world had no meaning, and I was readily able to find satisfactory grounds for this assumption. . . . For me, as it undoubtedly was for most of my generation, the philosophy of meaninglessness was an instrument of liberation from a certain moral system. We were opposed to morality because it interfered with our sexual freedom.

Huxley's confession sheds light on the otherwise inexplicable refusal

---

[27]   New York Times Magazine, June 25, 1978

[28]   Dr. Paul Forchheimer in *Living Judaism* (Phillip Feldheim, New York, 1983)

[29]   Confessions of a Professional Free Thinker, June 1966, Pg. 19

of many scientists to draw logical conclusions from a wealth of data implying the existence of a Creator. Not every scientist is as intellectually honest as Professor Flew. Consider, for example, the self-contradictory stance of leading evolutionist, Professor George Wald (Nobel Laureate in Physiology, 1967). Writing about the enormous complexity of organic molecules, Dr. Wald states:[30]

> To make an organism requires not only a tremendous variety of these substances, in adequate amounts and proper proportions, but also the right arrangement of them. The most complex machine man has devised—say an electronic brain—is child's play compared with the simplest of living organisms. The especially trying thing is that complexity here involves such small dimensions. It is on the molecular level; it consists of a detailed fitting of molecule to molecule such as no chemist can attempt. . . .

> The reasonable view was to believe in spontaneous generation; the only alternative was to believe in a single, primary act of supernatural creation. There is no third position. For this reason many scientists a century ago chose to regard the belief in spontaneous generation as a "philosophical necessity." . . .

> One has only to contemplate the magnitude of this task to concede that the spontaneous generation of a living organism is impossible. Yet here we are—as a result, I believe, of spontaneous generation.

The illogic of Dr. Wald's statement is surpassed only by the fantastic theory developed by Dr. Francis Crick, who won the Nobel Prize for discovering the double-helical structure of DNA. Faced with the prospect of admitting the miraculous origin of life, Dr.

---

[30]   *The Origin Of Life*, Scientific American, Volume 191, No. 4, Pg. 46

Crick, together with Dr. Leslie Orgel, Nobel Prize laureate Dr. Fred Hoyle, and Dr. Chandra Wickramasinghe came up with a theory, which apparently was more tenable to the scientists than the existence of God. Crick and his colleagues postulated that beings from another solar system had deposited on planet earth the building blocks of life (which, it was obvious to them, could not have self-generated through evolution). They called their theory "Directed Panspermia." This theory holds that: "Some extraterrestrial civilization of another solar system, because of the fear of extinction, decided to 'fertilize' other planets. They sent frozen bacteria to earth that evolved into life, as we know it."[31]

Dr. Crick then spelled out the moral ramifications of his theory. In a speech he inferred that "we cannot continue to regard all human life as sacred."[32] While careful to assert that he was not advocating the following ideas, but merely indicating the kind of ways in which society may be forced to reconsider conventional ethics, he declared:

> The idea that every person has a soul and that his life must be saved at all costs should not be allowed; instead, the status of birth and death should be reconsidered. If for example, a child was considered legally born when two days old, it could be examined to determine whether it was an "acceptable member of human society." It might also be desirable to define a person as legally dead when he was past the age of 80 or 85, and then expensive medical equipment should be forbidden him; old people might also be required to distribute a certain proportion of their property.

Furthermore, Dr. Crick felt that so important is it to understand the genetics of human endowment that parents should be permitted to dedicate one of a pair of identical twins to society so that the two twins could be brought up in different environments and compared. These

---

31   Directed Panspermia, Icarus, Volume 19, 1973, p. 341

32   *The Logic of Biology* (Nature, Volume 220, November 1968, pages 429-430)

ideas, as immoral as they sound, are the logical consequences of any "origin of life" theory that does not include God.

Another Nobel Laureate in Chemistry, Professor Harold S. Urey, admits that belief in evolution is akin to religious dogma:[33]

> Every scientist who investigates the origins of life discovers that the deeper we penetrate into this subject the more we suspect that it is impossible that such complexity could have been the result of accidental evolution . . . Nonetheless, we have unanimously agreed, as an article of faith, that life on this planet evolved from inert matter, even though the complexity of life forms is of such great magnitude that it is difficult to imagine how it all happened.

Conclusion

We have presented conclusive evidence of a Super-Creator based on abstract, mathematical, and scientific proofs.

Scientific objectivity dictates to us that our inability to see God cannot influence a decision of whether or not He exists. In fact, we have never seen many of the phenomena that we believe to be factual. Yet, we know that these things exist.

For example, the scientific community knew of the existence of the planet Neptune long before any human being ever saw it. In the first half of the nineteenth century it was realized that Uranus traveled in its orbit in a way that could not be accounted for by Newton's Law of Universal Gravitation. The discrepancy was tiny but it threatened to destroy Newton's whole premise. Lucky for Newton, it was mathematically proven that the gravitational pull Uranus was experiencing must indicate that there is a planet neighboring Uranus. Independently, the British John C. Adams, in 1845, and the French Le Verrier, in 1846, calculated the position and the mass of this body. Eventually, it was telescopically proven by J. Gottfried Galle at the Berlin Observatory, based on La Verrier's calculations, that Neptune existed.

---

[33]   Christian Science Monitor, January 4, 1962

Many scientific facts, from black holes to quarks, are accepted as real based on abstract, mathematical, and scientific proofs alone, without anybody having actually seen them.

Five

Between Europe,
Asia, and Africa

The "Clockmaker Theory" asserts that God created the world, but is not actively involved in its operation, just as a clockmaker makes a clock that then operates independently of him. Let's see if there's legitimacy to this claim.

In the words of famed nuclear physicist, Dr. Gerald Schroeder:

> I recently met in Jerusalem with Professor Leon Lederman, Nobel Prize winning physicist. We were talking science, obviously. And as the conversation went on, I said, "What about spirituality, Leon?" And he said to me, "Schroeder, I'll talk science with you, but as far as spirituality, speak to the people across the street, the theologians." But then he continued, and he said, "But I do find something spooky about the people of Israel coming back to the Land of Israel."

> Interesting . . . . Prof. Lederman found nothing spooky about the Eskimos eating fish at the Arctic Circle. And he found nothing spooky about Greeks eating Musika in Athens. But he finds something real spooky about Jews eating falafel on Jaffa Street.

Because it shouldn't have happened. It doesn't make sense
historically that the Jews would come back to the Land of Israel.
Yet that's what happened.

. . . . there is some monkey business going on with history that
makes it not all just random. That there's some direction to the
flow of history.[34]

King Frederick the Great once asked his Lutheran pastor to provide
him with a visible proof of God's existence. The pastor answered with
just two words: The Jews.

Samuel Clemens, better known as Mark Twain, wrote in 1898:

If the statistics are right, the Jews constitute but one per cent of
the human race. It suggests a nebulous dim puff of star-dust lost
in the blaze of the Milky Way. Properly the Jew ought hardly to
be heard of; but he is heard of, has always been heard of. He is as
prominent on the planet as any other people, and his commercial
importance is extravagantly out of proportion to the smallness
of his bulk. His contributions to the world's list of great names
in literature, science, art, music, finance, medicine, and abstruse
learning are also way out of proportion to the weakness of his
numbers.

He has made a marvelous fight in this world, in all the ages; and
has done it with his hands tied behind him. He could be vain of
himself, and be excused for it. The Egyptian, the Babylonian, and
the Persian rose, filled the planet with sound and splendor, then
faded to dream-stuff and passed away; the Greek and the Roman
followed, and made a vast noise, and they are gone; other peoples
have sprung up and held their torch high for a time, but it burned
out, and they sit in twilight now, or have vanished.

The Jew saw them all, beat them all, and is now what he always
was, exhibiting no decadence, no infirmities of age, no

---

34   Genesis & the Big Bang, (Bantam Books, 1991)

weakening of his parts, no slowing of his energies, no dulling of
his alert and aggressive mind. All things are mortal but the Jew;
all other forces pass, but he remains. What is the secret of his
immortality?[35]

Between 250 CE and 1948, a period of 1700 years, the Jews were
expelled from more than eighty countries. That's a new country
approximately every 22 years. To provide a few examples, the Jews
were expelled from England, France, Austria, Germany, Lithuania,
Spain, Portugal, Bohemia, and Moravia. History shows that a people
expelled from its land assimilates into the new land within three to four
generations. How is it possible that the Jews have continued to survive
as a distinct nation for over 2,000 years, and this despite not one, but
eighty expulsions?

The Bible predicts that the Jews will be expelled from the Land of
Israel, which will then become barren and desolate, but that the Jews
will later return to Israel. Both parts of this prediction fly in the face of
the norms of world history.

The Land of Israel is located at the meeting point of Europe, Asia,
and Africa. In ancient times, it was a highly prized trade route, leading
all the successive ancient empires (Egypt, Assyria, Babylonia, Persia,
Greece, Rome, etc.) to give high priority to conquering it. It was also
rich in olives (used for olive oil), grapes (used for wine), and other
agricultural crops. It is in the interests of conquering powers to colonize
and develop the lands they conquer, especially a land that is so
geographically important. Yet, after the Jews were expelled by the
Romans, the land fell into desolation for nineteen centuries, just as the
Bible prophesized.

Mark Twain traveled to Palestine in 1867. He described the utter
desolation and barrenness that he witnessed there:

> A desolate land whose soil, though more than sufficiently rich,
> produces only thorn bush and thistle—a silent mourning
> expanse. There is such desolation; one cannot even imagine
> that life's beauty and productivity once existed here . . . The

---

[35]   *Concerning the Jews*, Harper Magazine, March, 1898

Land of Israel dwells in sackcloth and ashes. The spell of a curse hovers over her, which has blighted her fields and imprisoned her mighty potential with shackles. The Land of Israel is wasteland, devoid of delight.[36]

Remarkably, as soon as the Jews returned, starting in the late 19th century, the land became fertile and reinvigorated.

The return of the Jewish people to their ancestral homeland after 1900 years is unprecedented in history, and can only be described as miraculous. Moreover, the achievement of the Jews of Israel since the establishment of the modern State of Israel fifty-eight years ago is beyond the norm of reason or logic. It is the 100th smallest country, with less than 1/1000th of the world's population, yet it boasts accomplishments that have changed the world:

- The cell phone, which today is viewed by most of the world community as "indispensable," was developed in Israel by the Israeli branch of Motorola, which has its largest development center in Israel.
- Every contemporary computer has Windows NT or XP. Most of these operating systems were developed by Microsoft-Israel. The Pentium MMX Chip technology was designed in Israel at Intel. Both the Pentium-4 microprocessor and the Centrino processor were entirely designed, developed, and produced in Israel. Voice mail technology was developed in Israel. Four young Israelis developed the technology for the AOL Instant Messenger ICQ in 1996.
- According to industry officials, Israel designed the airline industry's most impenetrable flight security. U.S. officials now look to Israel for advice on how to handle airborne security threats.
- Israel's $100 billion economy is larger than all of its immediate neighbors combined. Israel's GDP ranks number third among developing countries, following behind only Hong Kong and

---

36   *The Innocents Abroad*, Mark Twain, London 1881

Singapore. Israel has the highest percentage in the world of home computers per capita.

- Israel has the highest ratio of university degrees to the population in the world. Israel produces more scientific papers per capita than any other nation by a large margin—109 per 10,000 people—as well as one of the highest per capita rates of patents filed. Israel is ranked #2 in the world for venture capital funds, right behind the United States.

- On a per capita basis, Israel has the largest number of biotech startups.

- Israel has the world's second highest per capita of new books.

- Israel is the only country in the world that entered the 21st century with a net gain in its number of trees, made more remarkable because this was achieved in an area considered mainly desert.

- Israel has more museums per capita than any other country.

- Israel leads the world in the number of scientists and technicians in the workforce, with 145 per 10,000, as opposed to 85 in the U.S., over 70 in Japan, and less than 60 in Germany.

- Israeli innovations have had a major impact on the field of medicine: Israeli scientists developed the first fully computerized, no-radiation, diagnostic instrumentation for breast cancer. An Israeli company developed a computerized system for ensuring proper administration of medications, thus removing human error from medical treatment. (Every year in U.S. hospitals 7,000 patients die from treatment mistakes.) Israel developed the first ingestible video camera, so small it fits inside a pill. Used to view the small intestine from the inside, the camera helps doctors diagnose cancer and digestive disorders. Researchers in Israel developed a new device that directly helps the heart pump blood, an innovation with the potential to save lives among those with heart failure. The new device is synchronized with the heart's mechanical operations through a sophisticated system of sensors. A new acne treatment developed in Israel, the ClearLight device, produces a high-intensity, ultraviolet-light-free, narrow-band blue light that causes acne bacteria to self-destruct—all without damaging surroundings skin or tissue.

- An Israeli company was the first to develop and install a large-scale solar-powered and fully functional electricity generating plant, in southern California's Mojave Desert.
- On October 6, 2004, two Israeli scientists won the Nobel Prize in Chemistry for their research into ways that cells can shut down bad proteins and enzymes. This amazing research is being utilized to learn how to end the creation and proliferation of cancer cells and neurological disorders.

All the above was accomplished while engaged in intermittent wars with an implacable enemy that seeks its destruction, and an economy continuously strained by having to spend more per capita on its own protection than any other country on earth.

The Bible also prophesizes that the Jews will return to Israel en masse from the four corners of the world. In the last fifty years, Israel has absorbed Jewish immigrants from every continent and over seventy different countries. Israel, at the time of its inception in 1948, had a population of 600,000. Within its first five years, it absorbed 600,000 immigrants, doubling its own size. Relative to its population, Israel is the largest immigrant-absorbing nation on earth. In 1984 and again in 1991, Israel airlifted a total of 22,000 Ethiopian Jews to safety in Israel.

This entire sequence of events, prophesized in the Books of Ezekiel, Jeremiah, and Isaiah, defies nature, history, and logic.

A brief overview of the history of modern Israel also reads like a litany of miracles:

On the very day in May 1948, that the modern state of Israel declared its independence, five Arab armies attacked. The incipient state of 600,000 Jews was surrounded and attacked by nations populated by 50 million Arabs. Azzah Pasha, then the Secretary General of the Arab League, proclaimed over the airwaves: "This will be a war of extermination, and a momentous massacre."

The British, who were in control of Palestine from 1917 until the day the Jewish state was declared, prohibited the Jews from acquiring arms or military training. Thus, the army whose job it was to resist the well-equipped, British-trained invading Arab armies was a rag-tag group, many of whom were Holocaust survivors who were sent into battle on the very day they landed in Israel.

Yet, the fledgling Jewish state miraculously survived the onslaught. In fact, when the armistice lines were drawn in January, 1949, the Jews had gained 21% more land than had been originally given to them in the United Nations partition plan.

Nineteen years later, a coalition of Egypt, Syria, Lebanon, and Jordan decided the time had come to annihilate the Jewish state. They were equipped with $3,000,000,000 of military aid from the Soviet Union. Egypt demanded that the United Nation's peace-keeping force stationed in Sinai leave, a demand to which they promptly complied. The four Arab armies then deployed on Israel's borders, backed up by the armies of Iraq, Algeria, Kuwait, and Sudan. President Nasser of Egypt then closed the Straits of Tehran, thus blocking all shipping to Israel's southern port of Eilat. This was an internationally recognized act of war.

Israelis, out-numbered and out-armed, listened to daily Arab broadcasts threatening to drive them into the sea. And who would stop them? Not one nation in the world was willing to stand behind Israel or provide them with arms. The mood in the young Jewish state was so despairing that when the Prime Minister Levi Eshkol addressed the nation, adjuring them to be strong, he himself broke down and wept.

Miraculously, the war that broke out was over in six whirlwind days. Instead of defeat, Israel scored a stunning victory. To everyone's consternation, the Jews had tripled their territory, and had regained, after 2,000 years, their holiest sites in Jerusalem, Hebron, and Bethlehem.

On October 6, 1973, Israel was again engaged in war. It was called the Yom Kippur war because most Israelis had been in their synagogues, fasting and praying when they were suddenly attacked. Egypt attacked the Sinai Peninsula and Syria attacked the Golan Heights. In total, eleven Arab nations attacked Israel. Remember that Israel is a country smaller than the state of New Jersey. Miraculously, the Jews gained all strategic locations, threatened Damascus, and headed for Cairo. Two major Arab nations were seriously threatened, so Russia called for peace. Israel survived yet another attempt at annihilation.

In 1991, Israel was threatened again, this time by Iraq. After Iraq's invasion of Kuwait, the United States attacked Iraq. Saddam Hussein vowed to "incinerate" Israel with his Scud missiles. While the United States ordered Israel to refrain from self-defense and retaliation, Iraq showered 39 Scud missiles on the most densely populated areas of Israel. Miraculously, only one Israeli was killed.

In the wake of this war, the prestigious scientific journal *Nature*,[37] as well as M.I.T.,[38] published articles trying to evaluate how Israel was spared massive tragedy. Scientifically and militarily, the casualties should have been far greater. In previous wars elsewhere in the world in which V-2 Scud missiles were launched, massive casualties ensued. Even during the Gulf War, one Iraqi Scud missile striking Dhahran, Saudi Arabia, killed 28 American soldiers.

Let's analyze the miracle of the Gulf War in Israel. In 1944, when Germany attacked London, the ratio of casualties was five deaths and eleven severe injuries per missile. In the Tehran War, 1980-88, Iraq launched Scud missiles against Iran. In this war, the ratio of casualties was approximately thirteen deaths and thirty severe injuries per missile. Relative to these statistics, Israel should have suffered between 195 and 507 total deaths from 39 Scuds. Instead, it suffered only one death. (The population differential was: Iran 300/hectare and London 43/ hectare. The population in Tel Aviv, which suffered the major brunt of the missile attacks, was 70/hectare. That's more than 1.6 times the amount of London!) In terms of severe injuries, Israel could have been expected to suffer between 429 and 1170 severe injuries from 39 Scud missiles. Instead, there were 230 injuries. Of these, ten were moderate, and only one was severe.

In Israeli television broadcasts after every missile attack, the fervently secular news reporters would again and again use the word, "miracle."

---

[37] *Why were the Casualties So Low, Nature,* 361, 293-296 (28 Jan 1993)

[38] *Casualties and Damage from Scud Attacks in the 19991 Gulf War* (MIT, Defense and Arms Control Studies, January, 1993)

Interestingly, West Point Military Academy, America's foremost Military school, in its courses on military strategy does not attempt to analyze Israel's wars. It omits them from its curriculum because they do not follow the normal laws of warfare.

Objectively, we must conclude that such miraculous events suggest Divine intervention in human affairs. God not only created the universe; God is still involved in its workings.

Six

Scientific Fallibility

O ur entire exercise in proving God's existence may have been an exercise in futility. Perhaps modern human beings, with their advanced science and technology, have no need of God or religion. In an age of cloning, when, it seems imminent, humans can create other humans, who needs God? In the age of objective scientific truth, who needs subjective religious axioms?

For the last three centuries, science has been the shining star on the stage of civilization, while religion has been relegated to crouching in the wings, like a discredited has-been. Appellations such as "superstitious," "old-fashioned," and "dogmatic" have been ascribed to religious doctrines, while science has been awarded the crown of proven, incontestable, objective truth.

But are the claims of science really so verified and verifiable? M.D. Tendler, Ph.D., a renowned biologist, declared:[39]

> . . . In science, the truth changes. The nature of science has a human factor of fallibility. And as technology and science hold hands and move forward, we face brand new truths. Science has

---

[39]   Quoted in YUToday (2004).

made me a liar. For decades, I taught the one-gene, one enzyme axiom of biochemistry. I taught there were around 100,000 genes. We're down to 35,000 now. And one gene has learned to make multiple enzymes.

For years scientists referred to what seemed to be vast amounts of purposeless human genetic material as "Junk DNA." They posited that this DNA was a kind of genetic filler that the process of evolution had blindly deposited inside us, taking up space for no particular reason. Then, suddenly, in the year 2002, further research revealed that this whole concept was patently false. As the *Washington Post* reported (December 5, 2002):

> The huge stretches of genetic material dismissed in biology classrooms for generations as "Junk DNA" actually contain instructions essential for the growth and survival of people and other organisms, and may hold keys to understanding complex diseases such as cancer, strokes, and heart attacks. . . . The new analysis shocked scientists.

Here is another example that challenges the concept of scientific "truth": Most researchers maintained that there are four basic tastes: *salt*, *sour*, *bitter*, and *sweet*, each detected by a different area of the tongue. Until a few years ago, nearly all physiology textbooks included a "tongue map," showing which areas are more sensitive to which tastes. Then physiological psychologist Linda Bartoshuk found that the map was based on a misleading graph published in 1942—and it was simply wrong. The four basic tastes can be detected at any spot on the tongue that has receptors, and differences among the areas are small. What was considered to be factual and indisputable was actually a gross error. This error was caught in 1993, after fifty-one years of fallacious scientific education to the masses.

Sometimes science is dead wrong. Because all life is water based, without water there is no life. The question was how long did it take for water to give forth life. Science believed that billions of years passed in which random reactions eventually caused water and rock to bear living organisms. This was in contradistinction to the Bible, which taught that life appeared *immediately* after liquid water formed on earth. This immediate conjunction of water and life had, for decades, evolutionary biologists maligning and debasing the Bible. The scientists had to stifle their glee when in the 1970's Professors E. Barghoorn and Stanley Tyler discovered micro-fossils of bacteria and algae in chert rocks (a form of silicon dioxide once considered an unlikely source of fossils) dated at 3.6 billion years old, just after the time when liquid water formed on earth. The Bible was correct all along. Life appeared very rapidly, not after billions of years.[40]

In the early part of the 20th century the British scientific community collaborated in perpetrating a fraud of monumental proportions. Paleontologists and anthropologists claimed to have discovered the ultimate proof that human beings evolved from apes. They discovered a skull of a hybrid human being and claimed that this was the "missing link"—the intermediate stage between the ape and the human. They called this new specie the Piltdown Man. Religious dogma came under fierce attack. It seemed conclusive that Darwin was right; the human being was just an evolved ape. It took over forty years (1954) until it was revealed that someone intent on misleading the public had simply amalgamated bones of the ape and human being, so it turned out that this great discovery for evolution was a fabrication, a terrible hoax.

In July 1998, the prestigious *National Geographic* magazine published a monumental article; *Dinosaurs Take Wing*, which at long last, definitively proved the truths of evolution. Evolutionary biologists were ecstatic. A fossil, named *Archaeoraptor liaoningensis,* was finally discovered that filled in the gaps in their popular "dinosaur to bird" scenario because it manifested the long, bony tail of dromaeosaurid dinosaurs along with the specialized shoulder and chest of birds. It matched the criteria that evolutionary biologists were always hoping for to prove that birds evolved from the dinosaur. The fossil was discovered at Xiasanjiazi in China's northeastern Liaoning Province, and appeared to have the body of a primitive bird with the teeth and tail of a small, terrestrial dinosaur or dromaeosaur. I feel a ting of

---

[40] For more on this subject please see Dr. Gerald Schroeder's books, *The Science of God* (Broadway Books, 1998) and *The Hidden Face Of God: Science Reveals the Ultimate Truth* (Free Press, 2002)

empathy for the pathetic turn of events when I relate this story, as it does not have a happy ending for some. Quite unfortunate for evolution religionists, it turns out the entire fossil was a fraud.

Dr. Storrs L. Olson, the eminent curator of birds at the prestigious Smithsonian Institution's National Museum of Natural History immediately recognized the scandal. In an "open letter" dated November 1, 1999, and addressed to Dr. Peter Raven, Secretary of the National Geographic Society Committee for Research and Exploration, Olson verbally castigated the Society, Dr. Raven, Christopher P. Sloan (author of the *National Geographic* article), and Bill Allen, the magazine's editor, for what he called "an all-time low for engaging in sensationalistic, unsubstantiated, tabloid journalism."

> Prior to the publication of the article "Dinosaurs Take Wing" in the July 1998 *National Geographic*, Lou Mazzatenta, the photographer for Sloan's article, invited me to the National Geographic Society to review his photographs of Chinese fossils and to comment on the slant being given to the story. At that time, I tried to interject the fact that strongly-supported alternative viewpoints existed to what *National Geographic* intended to present, but it eventually became clear to me that *National Geographic* was not interested in anything other than the prevailing dogma that birds evolved from dinosaurs.
>
> Sloan's article takes prejudice to an entirely new level and consists in large part of unverifiable or undocumented information that "makes" the news rather than reporting it. His bold statement that "we can now say that birds are theropods just as confidently as we say that humans are mammals" is not even suggested as reflecting the views of a particular scientist or group of scientists, so that it figures as little more than editorial propagandizing. This melodramatic assertion had already been disproven by recent studies of embryology and comparative morphology, which, of course, are never mentioned . . .

The hype about feathered dinosaurs in the exhibit currently on display at the National Geographic Society is even worse, and makes the spurious claim that there is strong evidence that a wide variety of carnivorous dinosaurs had feathers. A model of the undisputed dinosaur *Deinonychus* and illustrations of baby tyrannosaurs are shown clad in feathers, all of which is simply imaginary and has no place outside of science fiction.

The idea of feathered dinosaurs and the theropod origin of birds is being actively promulgated by a cadre of zealous scientists acting in concert with certain editors at *Nature* and *National Geographic* who themselves have become outspoken and highly biased proselytizers of the faith. Truth and careful scientific weighing of evidence have been among the first casualties in their program, which is now fast becoming one of the grander scientific hoaxes of our age . . . But it is certain that when the folly has run its course and has been fully exposed, *National Geographic* will unfortunately play a prominent but unenviable role in the book that summarizes the whole sorry episode.

National Geographic found itself in the embarrassing position of having to retract the entire article because, as it turned out, the *Archaeoraptor* fossil was a fake—a neatly contrived composite of a bird and a dinosaur tail! In the March 2000 issue of National Geographic, the magazine published a "letter to the editor" from Xu Xing, one of the scientists who first examined and discussed the fossil find.

After observing a new, feathered dromaeosaur specimen in a private collection and comparing it with the fossil known as *Archaeoraptor,* I have concluded that *Archaeoraptor* is a composite. The tail portions of the two fossils are identical, but other elements of the new specimen are very different from *Archaeoraptor,* in fact more closely resembling *Sinornithosaurus.* Though I do not want to believe it, *Archaeoraptor* appears to be composed of a dromaeosaur tail and a bird body.

Seven months later, the October 2000 issue of *National Geographic* contained a comprehensive article by veteran investigative reporter Lewis M. Simons, describing how this ridiculous hoax occurred. In his *National Geographic* article, Simons explained how farmers in many regions of China have made a very profitable hobby of selling the fossils they find. The only problem is that these farmers realize that fossil fanciers prefer specimens assembled and suitable for display. Therefore, on occasion the farmers will "doctor" the fossils to follow basic market economics and thus increase the value of their finds. *Archaeoraptor* actually "evolved" in a Chinese farmhouse where homemade paste was used to glue together two completely different fossils. The result was the now-famous (or infamous, as the case may be) "missing link" that allegedly had the body of a primitive bird with the teeth and the tail of a terrestrial dinosaur.

The saga finally ended in March 2001. In the March 29, 2001 issue of *Nature,* Timothy Rowe and his colleagues published the results of their X-ray computed tomography studies on the *Archaeoraptor* fossil. Their study documented the fact that "the *Archaeoraptor* slab was built in three layers," and concluded that *Archaeoraptor* represents two or more species and that it was assembled from at least two, and possibly five, separate specimens. Additional work in China verified that the tail is from an entirely different specimen, which has been described previously as a new species of dromaeosaur.

Elite Cheaters and Liars in Scientific Medical Research

In a survey on scientific research integrity published June 9, 2005 in the journal *Nature*, about 1.5 percent of 3,247 researchers who responded admitted to falsification or plagiarism. One in three admitted to some type of professional misbehavior.

In July, 2005 the Associated Press published a fascinating news story in this regard. Dr. Andrew Friedman was an associate professor of obstetrics, gynecology and reproductive biology at Harvard Medical School and chief of the department of reproductive endocrinology at Brigham and Women's Hospital. Friedman was a brilliant surgeon and researcher with a major skeleton in the closet. He feared that he was about to lose everything—his career, his family, the life he'd built—because his boss was coming closer and closer to the truth: For the past three years, Friedman had been faking—actually making up—data in some of the respected, peer-reviewed studies he had published in top medical journals.

"It is difficult for me to describe the degree of panic and irrational thought that I was going through," he would later tell an inquiry panel at Harvard.

On the night of his 12th wedding anniversary, March 13, 1995, he had been ordered by his department chair to clear up what appeared to be suspicious data.

He chose not to clear things up.

"I did something which was the worst possible thing I could have done," he testified.

As is noted in the Associated Press article, Dr. Friedman went to the medical room, and for the next three or four hours he pulled out permanent medical files of a handful of patients. Then, he covered up his lies, scribbling in the information he needed to support his study.

"I created data. I made it up. I also made up patients that were fictitious," he testified.

His case, recorded in a seven-foot-high stack of documents at the Massachusetts Board of Registration in Medicine, tells a story of one man's struggle with power, lies and the crushing pressure of academia.

As reported by the Associated Press (July 11, 2005), unfortunately, there are many such cases. Chris Pascal, director of the Federal Office of Research Integrity, said its 28 staffers and $7 million annual budget haven't kept pace with the allegations. The result: Only 23 cases were closed last year. Of those, eight individuals were found guilty of research misconduct. In the past 15 years, the office has confirmed about 185 cases of scientific misconduct.

In November, 2004, federal officials found that Dr. Ali Sultan, an award-winning malaria researcher at the Harvard School of Public Health, had plagiarized text and figures, and falsified his data—substituting results from one type of malaria for another—on a grant application for federal funds to study malaria drugs. When brought before an inquiry committee, Sultan tried to pin the blame on a postdoctoral student. Sultan resigned and is now a faculty member at Weill Cornell Medical College in Qatar, according to a spokeswoman there.

In 1974, Dr. William Summerlin, a top-ranking Sloan-Kettering Cancer Institute researcher, used a marker to make black patches of fur on white mice in an attempt to prove his new skin graft technique was working.

"Often we're confronted with people who are brilliant, absolutely incredible researchers, but that's not what makes them great scientists. It's the character," said Debbi Gilad, a research compliance and integrity officer at the University of California, Davis, which has taken a lead role on handling scientific misconduct.

Fraudulent Doctor Still at the Helm of Medical Decision Making

Aren't you dying to know what transpired with Dr. Andrew Friedman? In 1999, after successfully petitioning to get his license reinstated, Dr. Andrew Friedman went to work as senior director of clinical research at Ortho-McNeil Pharmaceutical Inc., a Johnson & Johnson company. The job, which he still has, involves designing and reviewing clinical trials for hormonal birth control, writing package insert labels and lecturing to doctors.

Mary Anne Wyatt, a retired biochemist in Natick, Mass., is one of several former patients who unsuccessfully sued him. She said:

"I think it's not at all surprising that a drug company would hire somebody who is very comfortable with hiding the effects of very dangerous drugs."

The medical scientific establishment seems to remain apathetic to scandalous practices. Ortho-McNeil spokeswoman Bonnie Jacobs said the company was well aware of Friedman's history when it hired him. According to Jacobs:

"He is an excellent doctor, an asset to our company."

We have conclusively proven that science is as fallible as any other area of human investigation. Sometimes mistakes are the result of simple negligence, as in the case of the tongue map, at times the mistake is the result of what was termed in the previous chapter "philosophical necessities," i.e. the scientists' own dogmatic resistance to drawing inferences that fly in the face of their cherished beliefs, while at other times scientists cheat and lie in order to advance in power and prestige. Whatever the cause, however, science cannot be the bearer of ultimate truth.

Playing God

Two stories: A gynecologist, while delivering a baby, realized that the child was deformed. For an instant he had a strong urge to asphyxiate the child and thus spare so much unnecessary anguish, expense, and effort, as would surely be the lot of this hapless child and her family. The doctor, an ethical man, overcame the temptation to play God, and the baby girl was delivered, with only one leg.

Many years later, this same doctor was attending a concert. He was particularly moved by the lovely and talented young woman who played the cello with such haunting poignancy and depth. He was so impressed that he inquired who the cellist was, only to discover that this woman was the baby whom he had almost prevented from taking her first breath.

The second story is about Dr. Kenneth Swan, a young army surgeon stationed in Vietnam. A horribly wounded, mangled nineteen-year-old soldier, Kenneth McGarity, was brought in off the battlefield and deposited in Dr. Swan's operating theater. A Viet Cong grenade had blown the soldier's legs off and blinded him. His life was hanging in the balance. The surgeon worked on McGarity for over seven hours, amputating his legs and operating on his arms and head. All his colleagues criticized him for treating the soldier, who they say would have been better off dead. Dr. Swan was filled with anguish and doubt about saving the soldier's life only to condemn him to a bitter shadow of an existence. After twenty-three years of guilt, Dr. Swan tracked down Kenneth McGarity, and found him a happily married man, the father of two daughters, who, despite being blind and paraplegic, had a positive attitude toward his life.

Theologian Zalman Posner wrote:

> Observable phenomena and measurable quantities are raw
> materials for the scientist—or for man, if you will. Before long it
> became evident that there are "things" which are not readily
> observable or subject to quantitative measurement. The scientist
> could deal with "what" happens and "how" but the "why" was
> beyond his purview. Right and wrong could not be tested,
> observed, or measured by any of his instruments, not even the
> philosopher's intellect. The scientist therefore concluded that
> he is in no position to make "value judgments." For him as a
> scientist there is no such thing as good or evil.

> Values persist, moral decisions continue to be made, but neither
> the scientists' laboratory, nor the philosopher's seminar offer
> guidance here. The scientist can explain how a heart is
> transplanted or how an atom bomb can be exploded, but he
> cannot tell us whether, morally, we are justified in doing these
> things. Today's secular philosopher does not concern himself
> with the classic problems of good and evil, not because he is
> indifferent, or because he feels that the problems have been
> resolved, but because his philosopher's tools are inadequate or
> inappropriate to the task. These particular concepts are outside
> his realm. Man does not possess the human resources to define
> or even justify morality as morality.[41]

I recently heard a scientific debate on the merit or demerit of
embryonic stem cell research. The debate revolved on the questions:
When does life for the fetus begin? When is it imbued with a soul?
These are questions that mortals, including scientists, cannot
answer.

As Joseph Wood Krutch, Ph.D., one of America's most
distinguished literary naturalists said: "Science can tell us how to do
more and more things; it cannot tell us what ought to be done."

---

[41] In *Think Jewish* (Kesher Publications, Nashville, Tennessee, 1978)

Science as the Complement of Religion

Some of the greatest scientists maintained that true science is actually the expression of God. Nobel Prize winning physicist Max Planck wrote:[42]

> There can never be any real opposition between religion and science; for the one is the complement of the other. Every serious and reflective person realizes that the religious element in his nature must be recognized and cultivated if all the powers of the human soul are to act together in perfect balance and harmony. And indeed it was not by any accident that the greatest thinkers of all ages were deeply religious souls . . . Science enhances the moral values of life . . . because every advance in knowledge brings us face to face with the mystery of our own being.

A truly religious person sees and feels God's presence through His creations. The perfect order of the planetary rotations, the intricacy of an orchid, the graceful leaps of an antelope—all pay homage to their Creator. The more a person understands the incredible design and interworkings of nature, the more s/he will appreciate the Designer. Yet, God is much greater than the sum total of nature. God exists in nature, but God is not limited to nature.

As nuclear physicist and spiritual sage, Aryeh Kaplan explains:

> In a simple sense, religion is the recognition of the fact that all creation is mysterious, that it points to an Ultimate, to an Eternal Mystery, beyond the material universe. The world in which we live is filled with depth and mystery, and this sense of mystery in the universe is akin to the instinct of religion. The poet, the artist, the musician, the philosopher, the scientist, and the scholar—indeed, every person who seeks truth or beauty, is searching for God, whether he knows it or

---

[42] *Where is Science Going?* (London, 1933 pp, 168-169)

not. If he could only realize that this all-pervading mystery is a purposeful Being, then the research of the scientist and the rapture of the poet would become religious experiences.[43]

From the tiniest cell in protoplasm to the great trunk of a huge redwood tree, everything attests to God's greatness and being. As my former professor, Dr. Anthony J. Tolvo, a researcher at Rockefeller University, wrote me:

> A single cell is actually a factory with an intricate, complex system. Theories such as natural selection are immediately dispelled by observation of the cell. How much more so when we observe a conglomeration of cells, such as a person or an animal—or, for that matter, anything in nature. Science deals with the concrete: the observable, that which can be documented. Deductions and inferences are made about the world about us. The most abstract concepts of astrophysics are derivations of the visible, tangible world. Albert Einstein could not have imagined a relativistic universe were it not for the fact that he was able to make logical extensions of his visible world into an abstract realm. Thus, the basic theorems of science are based on initial visible observations: The train whistle that changes in pitch as it approaches an observer and passes him by: Doppler Effect!
>
> As a biologist, I am constantly astounded by the beauty and intricacy of what I see in the visible world around me. For one to argue that our existence is the sum of an unavoidable series of mathematical theorems (we are a consequence of chaos mathematics!) is nonsense! The basic structure of the universe, the structure of life, my neuronal manipulations as I write this to you are nothing short of miracles..

---

[43]   *Facets and Faces* (Moznaim Publications, New York, 1993)

Seven

Religion the Cop-Out

K arl Marx said, "Religion is the opiate of the masses." Is it true? Is religion just a crutch for weak-minded people who cannot take control of their own lives?

Actually, recent scientific studies have shown just the opposite. Marx defined religion as a security blanket, akin to a dependency on drugs, but studies now show that religious people are <u>less</u> apt to depend on drugs than non-religious people and are more apt to take control of their lives.

A recent study conducted by Dr. Ariel Knafo at Israel's Ben-Gurion University, in conjunction with the American Organization for Psychological Study and Social Issues, surveyed juniors and seniors in twenty government schools, both religious and secular, throughout Israel. The study found a significant connection between students' values and their likelihood of using drugs. Students who held "conservative" values—such as respect for parents, tradition, security, self-discipline, and care for others—were less likely to use drugs than those who valued personal freedom and independence. In addition, the study found that in schools that promote security, harmony, understanding and goodwill, there was less of a tendency to depend on hallucinogenic substances than in those that don't. As a result, the study found that students in religious schools were less likely to use drugs than those in secular schools.

Similarly, Columbia University's National Center on Addiction and Substance Abuse found that religiously engaged teens are far less likely to use drugs. According to the study: "Teens who attend religious services at least once a week are at significantly lower risk of substance abuse."

Religion also works wonders in rehabilitating addicts. Dr. Ur Timor, of the Department of Criminology and the Interdisciplinary Department of Social Science at Bar-Ilan University, wrote his doctoral thesis on the affect of introducing Jewish observance as a facilitator to rehabilitating criminals, most of whom are also drug addicts. He found that rehabilitation is really a process of changing the convict's value system. Dr. Timor contrasted the convicts' previous secular lives with Judaism: "Their lives as criminals, according to their own descriptions, were based on immediate gratification and extreme pursuit of pleasure. Judaism sees in the material world only a milestone on the path to a spiritual life."

Sara Zaltsberg wrote her graduate thesis in criminology on newly-observant Jews and drug rehabilitation. As part of her study, she interviewed former addicts. Many of the addicts had come to realize that the pleasure derived from drugs is unfulfilling. One former addict said, "I had everything. I was spoiled. I had women, money, cars—but in reality I had nothing. Everything was passing and impermanent." Another addict said, "Once I thought that I should spend my time doing the white stuff, discos, and women. Every week I would change women. I know that world, and I know it can only offer emptiness and stupidity." And yet another addict: "Slowly we saw the fakeness of it. You don't fool anyone. Girls, drugs—everything is external. Nothing lasts. In Judaism there is a higher power that wants you to rise and advance spiritually." Another addict confided, "I stole money to get drugs. When you are on drugs you don't care about anything. You are even willing to kill your own brother for drugs."

Zaltsberg attests: "My study found that the process of becoming newly religious and entering into a religious framework make a significant contribution to rehabilitation from drug addiction. The opinion among all the subjects studied was that Judaism is a constructive force, and a major factor in the success of the addicts' attempt to free themselves from drug abuse."

The same is true for dependence on alcohol. In March 1976, then-commissioner Jerome Hornblass of the NYC Addiction Services Agency called attention to data that showed that Jews with a strong commitment to their religion had very low rates of alcoholism. Among irreligious, assimilated Jews, however, rates had become virtually the same as those among non-Jews. Similar findings have been published in a study entitled "How Jews Avoid Alcohol problems" by the *American Sociological Review*.[44]

The dynamic of the soul's coming to faith is masterfully portrayed in the classic *The Devil's Advocate*. In this best-selling book, memoirs written by the mysterious character Giacomo Nerone testify to his spiritual struggle:

> To be born into the church is at once a burden and a comfort. The burden of ordinance and prohibition and, later, of belief. The comfort comes afterwards, when one begins to ask questions and is presented with a key to every problem of existence. Make the first conscious act of faith; accept the first premise, and the whole logic falls into place. One may sin, but one sins inside a secure cosmos. One is constrained to repentance by the sheer order of it. When Catholics become jealous of unbelievers, as they often do, it is because the burden of belief is heavy and the constraints chafe. Some end by rejecting the belief—as I did. . . . If one rejects it, one is lost . . . .

> I was lost a long time without knowing it. Without the faith, one is free of its inflexible constraints, and that is pleasant at first. Later, the terror comes. One is free—but free in chaos, in an unexplainable world, from which there is no retreat but inward, toward the hollow core of oneself. I think, therefore I am, Descartes said. But what am I? An accident going no place.

---

[44]   Volume 40, pages 646-672

How does one come back to belief out of unbelief? Out of sin, it is easy; a repentant child returns to a Father. In unbelief there is no Father. One comes from nowhere, goes nowhere. One's noblest acts are robbed of meaning. I tried to reason myself back to a first cause, as a foundling might reason himself back to his father, since all children have fathers. But who was He? Did He love me—or had He forgotten me forever? This was the real terror, and, as I look back on it now, from the security I have reached, I tremble and I sweat and I pray desperately: "Hold me close. Never let me go again. Never hide your face from me. It is terrible in the dark!"

If one's ultimate value is personal freedom, then religion, with its obligations and restrictions, is clearly to be avoided. Many thinking people, however, realize that the benefits of religion, in terms of a meaningful and ethical life, are worth the sacrifice.

From my own standpoint, even if there were no such idea as organized religion and no obligation to practice religion, I believe that I would still choose to be religious. This may seem a bit absurd because one would think that without religion I would be less cumbered and free—enjoying a life without any restrictions or limitations. No directions or responsibilities. Yet contrary to these expectations, and I must say I am surprised myself, I would imagine life absent of religion as stripped of genuine meaning. Religion directs people to be responsible for their actions and deeds, to accord value and dignity to all creations, and to be gracious, generous, and kind. Additionally, religion molds me into a better person by teaching me that I am on this world to have a positive affect on mankind. My religious convictions help me achieve these goals by providing me with rules of conduct to aid me in differentiating between right and wrong.

Far from being a crutch for the weak, religion can engender strength, discipline, and ethical behavior. It also gives people a wellspring of hope and joy. In contrast, Marx, the father of Communism, the most failed and expensive (in terms of millions of lives) social experiment in modern times, was a staunch Darwinist and atheist. He believed that there are no moral absolutes, no right and wrong. According to Marx, man is without soul, spirit, or free will and is not responsible for his own acts. Marx further believed that man is an economically determined animal. This meant that qualities of human intelligence, personality, emotional and religious life, merely reflect man's economic environment and the evil a man does is simply a reflection of his environment.

Marx himself was true to his contentions. He eschewed the "virtues and values that originate with God," and ended up having an illicit affair with his family's servant girl. When the girl became pregnant, Marx avoided taking responsibility, and even got his single friend Engels to pretend that he was the father. The servant girl, who had been in the employ of the family since her teens, remained with the Marx family, but the child was banished. When the boy grew up, Marx continued to shun him and would not even allow him to visit his mother using the front steps of the Marx house. As historian Paul Johnson points out, despite all of Marx's lofty writings sympathizing with the plight of the proletarians, the servant woman and her son with Marx were probably the only proletarians Marx knew personally, and he treated them despicably.[45]

A recent column by journalist Larry Derfner, who describes himself as "a secular leftist," contrasts the level of altruism between religious, right-wing Israeli settlers and secular, left-wing Israeli intellectuals:

> I ask myself: If I were stranded in the desert and only one car was going to come by, who would I prefer to be in it—a family of religious settlers from Beit El or a post-Zionist Ph.D. student from Tel Aviv University? There's no question.

> When it comes to going out of their way to help others, the settlers are just world-beaters, while leftists live their own lives, they're individualists, they like their privacy to think their own thoughts.

> Giving of yourself to help the other guy is supposed to be a core value of the Left. Who lives it, and who doesn't?[46]

---

[45]   Paul Johnson, *Intellectuals* (Harper & Row, 1988)

[46]   The Jerusalem Post, January 13, 2005

The benefits of religion are not only in the moral and psychological spheres. Evidence shows that religion may confer longer life and better health. Bnei Brak, a city with almost exclusively religious inhabitants, has the highest average life expectancy in Israel. What makes this finding even more astounding is that Bnei Brak is also Israel's poorest and most crowded city, thus confounding the expected correlation between increased wealth and health. Moreover, as journalist Jonathan Rosenblum notes, rates of smoking among males in Bnei Brak remain high, and even a casual glance around the streets of Bnei Brak will serve to establish that news of the benefits of exercise and a low-fat diet has not yet reached most of its inhabitants.

Rosenblum, writing in the *Jerusalem Post* (February 28 2002), reports other related and surprising discoveries:

- A Duke University study showed that those who attend religious services once a week are half as likely to have elevated blood levels of interleukin-6, which is associated with some cancers and heart disease.
- One California study conducted over 28 years and published in 1997, found that those who attended religious services weekly had a one-third lower death rate.
- A 1995 Dartmouth Medical School study of 232 patients recovering from open-heart surgery found that none of the 37 patients who described themselves as deeply religious died over the first six months, while 10% of the rest did. Those who received strong community support reinforced by strong religious belief were 14 times as likely to survive as those who had neither. Even when a strong community support structure is kept constant, religious belief appears to have an independent salutary effect.
- A study comparing residents of secular kibbutzim with those of religious communities in Israel over 16 years found that the religious communities had consistently lower mortality rates for the entire period.

It seems irrefutable that religion yields benefits to those who espouse it. But, given the plethora of religious beliefs and dogmas, how can we know which one to follow?

Eight

Absolutism

Now that we have established that the human being has a soul endowed with free will to choose between right and wrong, we must address the issue: How is one to know what is right and what is wrong?

The two answers most commonly given for this conundrum are: 1) Genetics (heeding your conscience) and 2) Follow an ethical system. Let's examine these two possibilities.

Katherine Hobson in *U.S. News & World Report* (2/28/05) notes that if asked if it would ever be OK to kill your own child, you don't have to think very hard before answering, "No." And no matter what arguments someone offered, you would probably wince at the idea that even consensual, safe sex between siblings is anything but bad.

Jonathan Haidt, a psychology professor at the University of Virginia, believes these initial reactions are based on five intuitions, deep-wired in the brain by eons of evolution. Cultural norms and practices are based on these instincts, he says, much as cuisines are built on the five taste receptors. According to Haidt, who happens to be a very respected author and scientist, your moral choices are based on the evolution of your genes.

Harvard biologist Edward O. Wilson, in his acclaimed work *Sociobiology,*[47] claims that incest is taboo because of the heavy physiological penalty imposed by inbreeding: "It results in children who are diminished in overall body size, muscular coordination, and academic performance. Throughout most of the history of human evolution, sociobiologists point out, humans did not have any knowledge of genetics. Thus, 'the gut feeling' that promotes sanctions against incest is largely unconscious. Individuals with a strong disposition to avoid incest passed on more of their genes to the next generation because their children were less likely to suffer the illness from inbreeding. And over many centuries of natural selection of individuals who did not inbreed, humans developed an instinct, which is based on genes."

Scientists have refuted the theory that genes definitively mold character and *dictate* moral choices[48]. To demote our moral choices to genes and evolution is equivalent to claiming that we humans are mere animals with limited intelligence. The logical deduction of such a theory is to abdicate personal responsibility for our moral choices. No act can be considered significantly premeditated.

The conscience of any individual is shaped by parents and society. The scion of a Mafia family will believe that murder is perfectly legitimate whenever someone interferes with the welfare or profit of the Family. Children growing up in the Palestinian Authority today are taught that the noblest goal they can aspire to is to become a *shaheed*— a suicide bomber who kills unarmed men, women, and children in order to further their nationalistic cause. The conscience of any individual is only as moral as the parental and societal forces that shaped it.

The same problem applies when we consider ethical systems. In 1831, Charles Darwin accompanied Captain Robert FitzRoy on

---

[47] 1979, pp. 38-40

[48] See for example research done by Professor Richard C. Lewontin et al., *Not in Our Genes: Biology, Ideology and Human Nature* (Pantheon, New York, 1984), Professor William Byne (1995) and Professor L. Peplau et al., *Close Relationships: a Sourcebook* (Sage, Thousand Oaks, Ca., 2000). Also, world famous cognitive psychologist and professor, Dr. Reuven Feuerstein is renown for his monumental work in proving that genes don't dictate intelligence or ability.

a royal expedition aboard His Majesty's ship, the Beagle. Their objective was to explore various lands in Latin America. During their voyage to the Straits of Magellan, they observed the natives of Tierra del Fuego. Darwin writes of one crewmember's observations in his journal:[49]

Was a more horrid deed ever perpetrated, then that witnessed . . . by Byron [a ship's officer], who saw a wretched mother pick up her bleeding dying infant-boy, whom her husband had mercilessly dashed on the stones for dropping a basket of eggs!

Apparently, in the ethical system of the Fuegians, killing a child for dropping a basket of eggs was perfectly acceptable. That it seemed culpable to the British officer and to Darwin was a statement of how much their ethical system differed. But who is to say that Western European society is any more "right" in absolute terms than the society of Tierra del Fuego? As sociologist William Kornblum points out, "But norms are never absolute. There are almost always conditions under which they may be violated. Thus, the same British seamen who were shocked to hear of a father killing his infant son might not be shocked at the news of Britons killing natives in other parts of England's far flung empire."[50]

As Professor Lawrence Kelemen has written:

> There are many societies besides ours. What makes the West a moral authority over certain Eastern and African civilizations that condone infanticide, cannibalism, and other murderous behaviors? Is it logical that one group of people should dictate morality to all the others just because they speak the most articulate English or earn the highest per capita income or boast the highest geographical density of fast-food restaurants?[51]

---

[49]   The Voyage of the Beagle, 1860, page 217. Incidentally, for similar reasons, Captain FitzRoy, on an earlier expedition, kidnapped some natives and brought them to England to "civilize" them. He hoped to later re-introduce them to their societies and they would be able to implement change. His experiment failed.

[50]   *Sociology in a Changing World* (Winston, 1988)

[51]   *Permission to Believe* (Targum Press, 1991), p. 24.

Not only do the ethical values of various societies differ, but also there may be major inconsistencies within the values of any one society. For example, when the Spanish conquistadors came to Tenochtitlan, now known as Mexico City, they found that the Aztecs were practicing human sacrifice and cannibalistic rituals. The Spanish, of course, considered these practices savage and deplorable. At the very same time, however, the Spanish Inquisition, in which "heretics" were tortured and publicly burned at the stake, was in full swing, with the endorsement of the Spanish crown and the enthusiastic approval of the Spanish masses, for whom the *auto-da-fe* was a beloved spectator sport.

The contemporary response to such societal differences is to conclude that, in the absence of an absolute moral standard, only relative ethics apply. According to this viewpoint, it is imperialism to tell a cannibal that his/her time-honored ethos is wrong, or to tell a Muslim fundamentalist that *jihad* (killing non-believers for the sake of Allah) is immoral. "One man's terrorist is another man's freedom fighter."

"Relative ethics," however, is an oxymoron. The definition of "ethic" is: A set of principles of right conduct.[52] To the extent that such principles are fluid and can be changed according to the time, place, and situation, to that extent they are useless in defining a standard of right conduct. Relative ethics leads directly to the conviction that adultery is wrong, until I desire my friend's wife; theft is wrong, until I need money and you have an abundance.

The world has a system of standard weights and measures because during the Middle Ages in the town of Troyes, France, set standards of weights and measures were kept. People from all over Europe who came to the annual fair in Troyes took duplicates of these standards home with them. Imagine if a citizen of Rome had declared that a pound in Troyes was a bit too heavy; he preferred a lighter pound for Roman standards. A "standard weight" that is not universally accepted is meaningless as a standard weight.

---

[52]   Excerpted from The American Heritage® Dictionary of the English Language, Third Edition © 1996 by Houghton Mifflin Company. Electronic version licensed from INSO Corporation; further reproduction and distribution in accordance with the Copyright Law of the United States. All rights reserved.

Variability in weights and measures renders them useless. Variability in ethics renders them absurd and irrelevant.

An archer once took his friend to the forest to show off his skill in archery. The friend was amazed to see that on dozens of targets drawn on the trees the archer's arrow had hit the bull's-eye, without a single miss. "How did you do it?" the friend asked.

"It was easy," replied the archer. "First I shot the arrow, then I drew the target around it."

Using relative ethics, anyone can be virtuous and moral. "Here's what I do," declares the relative ethicist, "and here's the system of morality, newly drawn up for the occasion, that defines my action as 'on target.'"

Using such relative ethics, even Heinrich Himmler, Hitler's notorious deputy and the head of the SS and the Gestapo, which oversaw the systematic extermination of millions of innocent people, was able to define himself as "good." Himmler was keenly interested in religion. According to Walter Schellenberg, "Himmler had the best and richest library on the Jesuit Order, whose literature he perused at night for years. Thus he built up his SS organization according to Jesuit principles."[53] He was also well versed in Eastern religion, particularly Buddhism. He believed that every cause has its ideal of sacrifice, which requires the individual to give up his well being for the sake of something greater. In a famous speech to his SS officers during the period they were running the concentration camps, Himmler declared: "To have stuck it out, and at the same time . . . to have remained decent fellows—that is what has made us hard."

Himmler once told his masseur, Dr. Felix Kersten: "A man has to sacrifice himself even though it is often very hard for him; he ought not to think of himself. . . . I try to reach a compromise in my own life; I try to help people and do good, relieve the oppressed and remove injustices whenever I can."[54]

---

[53] *Hitler's Secret Service* (Pyramid Publications, New York, 1974)

[54] *The Memoirs of Dr. Felix Kersten* (Doubleday & Co. New York, 1947)

With the Best of Intentions

Himmler may be an extreme example of evil deluding itself and posing as good. A famous experiment conducted by Yale psychology professor Stanley Milgram, however, demonstrated that 65% of "normal people" would kill for no good reason. In 1961-62, Professor Milgram conducted a series of experiments at Yale. He found, surprisingly, that 65% of his subjects, ordinary residents of New Haven, were willing to give apparently harmful electric shocks-up to 450 volts-to a pitifully protesting victim, simply because a scientific authority commanded them to, and in spite of the fact that the victim did not do anything to deserve such punishment. The victim was, in reality, a good actor who did not actually receive shocks, and this fact was revealed to the subjects at the end of the experiment.

As Milgram wrote of his findings:

> Many subjects will obey the experimenter no matter how vehement the pleading of the person being shocked, no matter how painful the shocks seem to be, and no matter how much the victim pleads to be let out. This was seen time and again in our studies and has been observed in several universities where the experiment was repeated. . . .

> A commonly offered explanation is that those who shocked the victim at the most severe level were monsters, the sadistic fringe of society. But if one considers that almost two-thirds of the participants fall into the category of "obedient" subjects, and that they represented ordinary people drawn from working, managerial, and professional classes, the argument becomes very shaky. . . .

> Sitting back in one's armchair, it is easy to condemn the actions of the obedient subjects. But those who condemn the subjects measure them against the standard of their own ability to formulate high-minded moral prescriptions. That is hardly a fair standard. Many of the subjects, at the level of stated opinion,

feel quite as strongly as any of us about the moral requirement
of refraining from action against a helpless victim. They, too, in
general terms know what ought to be done and can state their
values when the occasion arises. This has little, if anything, to
do with their actual behavior under the pressure of
circumstances.[55]

Milgram found that 100% of his subjects were willing to apply electric
shocks to the "victim" strapped into a chair, despite the "victim's"
protestations. At some point in the experiment, 35% of the subjects refused
to continue. Another 65% did continue, going so far as to press the red
lever labeled, "Danger! High Voltage!" thus ostensibly "killing" the victim.

Milgram framed the implications of his experiment in terms of blind
obedience to authority, but they are just as alarmingly a proof of the
consequences of relative ethics. Not one single subject refused to press
the first lever, supposedly administering a low level of electric shock,
despite the fact that, "they, too, in general terms know what ought to
be done and can state their values when the occasion arises."

What if one of Milgram's subjects had subscribed to a system of
absolute morality that absolutely forbade hurting other people except
for their own benefit (such as in medical surgery)? A person who
subscribed to absolute morality would have refused to press even the
first lever. Milgram proved that relative morality cannot stop ordinary,
decent people, who generally believe that it is wrong to inflict pain on
others, from doing just that!

The problem of relative ethics can work in the opposite direction as
well. If a person aspires to do good, what are the parameters and limits
that must guide such benevolence? The case of Zell Kravinsky is instructive
here. Dr. Kravinsky taught Renaissance History at the University of
Pennsylvania. Clearly, he has an astute intellect. After making multi-millions
in commercial real estate, Dr. Kravinsky decided that in order for one to
attain true fulfillment in one's life, one has to be a giver.

He decided to give away the bulk of his fortune to the needy. As a
result, he and his family lived almost as paupers. Then he heard about

---

55   Stanley Milgram, *Obedience to Authority*, (Harper & Row, 1974) pp. 3-7.

the plight of a young woman in dire need of a kidney transplant. He volunteered to donate his kidney to her. Dr. Kravinsky recently made a statement that in the event that he can be matched again as a donor, he would donate his second kidney, which would spell his own death. His wife, a psychiatrist, branded him "crazy" and threatened divorce.

Would Dr. Kravinsky be acting morally to donate his second kidney to a deserving recipient? Most people would agree that altruism is a positive virtue, but how far should it be taken? Without absolute morality it would be hard to define the limits of altruism. In fact, in this case God's law states that a person cannot forfeit his or her own life for the life of another human being.

Is humanity thus left with no absolute ethical standard? We have established that humans are defined by their Divine souls, and that the definitive characteristic of the soul is its ability to choose freely between good and evil. Would the God who created such souls thus leave them adrift in a sea of moral uncertainty, without revealing to them the good He wishes them to choose and the evil he wishes them to spurn? This would be akin to receiving the gift of a shiny new Lexus—set down in jungle where there are no roads on which to drive it.

Logic suggests that God, who wants us to choose good, must have revealed to us what constitutes good. Does such an absolute, God-given code of conduct exist? For over 3,300 years, the Jewish people has claimed to have been given such a code, called the Torah, a Hebrew word that means "instruction, guidance, or teaching."

As two contemporary writers wrote:

If man ultimately determines good and evil, then he stands as it were, above ethics—beyond the concepts of good and evil, which he himself created. If humans define morality, it can also be put aside for various human needs. Man is at liberty to tinker with his inventions. Divine morality, however, stands eternally. Ordained by Him, Who created both man and the world, this morality transcends the vicissitudes of mortal whims. It is forever valid, and man accepts it upon himself in reverence and awe.[56]

---

[56] Y. Schwartz and Y. Goldstein in *Shoah* (Mesorah Publications, New York, 1990) translated by Shlomo Fox-Ashrei

Absolute Morality in Action

Let's consider how such absolute morality would determine one's actions in a case where one's "feelings" would be a poor guide to true morality: Alvin was driving down the highway. He noticed two cars sitting on the shoulder with their distress signals on. The drivers of both cars were peering over the hoods of their respective cars. As Alvin slowed down and looked more intently, he realized that he recognized both drivers. One was his friend and current business partner; the other was his long-time nemesis and current business rival. Alvin pulled over and helped his friend fix his car, ignoring his enemy.

Was Alvin right? What would you have done?

If guided by your own feelings, you would have done as Alvin did. The Torah, however, mandates a different course of action. It states: "If you see the donkey of someone you hate crouching under its burden, would you refrain from helping him?—You shall help repeatedly with him."[57]

Commenting on this verse, the Talmud teaches that if one finds both his good friend and his foe in the same predicament, he must first go to the assistance of the foe, in order to subdue the evil inclination that encourages one to let an enemy suffer.

Let us take this a step further. Imagine being in the Peace Corp in a third-world country. You see that one of the natives is *loading* his donkey, while another person is *unloading* his donkey. Which of the two people should you help first? God's law states that you should first help the person *unloading* his animal. Why? In order to alleviate the prolonged pain the animal might suffer from carrying its burden.

With this piece of information at hand, what is the moral course of action if, still in the third-world country, you come to a dirt road where you discover two locals who are familiar to you. One is a friend and the other a foe. Your friend is *unloading* his donkey, while your foe is *loading* his donkey. You have learned that it is imperative to help your enemy before your friend. You have also learned that the appropriate behavior is to help somebody *unload* before helping somebody *load*. What do you do in this case?

---

[57]   Exodus, 22:5

The Talmud ordains that you should help your enemy load first. In this case, God considers the reconciliation of enemies' paramount and above the concern for the animal's lengthened discomfort.

Let us now consider one more version of this situation. Let's say you encounter your enemy with his car broken down by the side of the highway. You pull over, get out of your car, and offer to help him change his tire. The fellow hands you the jack and lies down on the grass. What should you do in this case? Some ethicists may recommend that despite the driver's audacity, you still attempt to help him. God says otherwise. According to God's law, if the owner refuses to help and expects the passerby to do it himself, the passerby is excused from helping, because the Torah qualified the commandment by saying that it must be performed "*with him*."[58]

It is clear from the above that although a person may have the right intentions and behave with a generous spirit, without the benefit of the absolute morality of the Torah, it would be impossible to accurately know how to act.

As Dr. J.H. Hertz, former Chief Rabbi of Great Britain, expressed it: "The will of God revealed in His Torah is the one eternal and unfailing guide as to what constitutes good and evil—and not man's instincts, or even his reason, which in the hour of temptation often call light darkness and darkness light."[59]

Morality Misconceptions

Rabbi Elijah of Vilna, a great sage of two centuries ago, explains that a person must learn to control his feelings and emotions, and direct them according to the teachings of God as recorded in the Torah. Sometimes a person is challenged in the very character trait that is his trademark. For example, the patriarch Abraham was known for his kindness. All of the Biblical stories relating to him portray Abraham as the epitome of kindness. The climax of his personal growth came when God commanded him to sacrifice his son Isaac. This test, which

---

[58]   Talmud, Baba Metzia 32b-33a

[59]   In *The Pentateuch* (Soncino Press, London, 1975) p. 8

demanded from Abraham cruelty, the opposite of kindness, took him
to the apex of his spiritual evolution. He proved that just as his kindness
was according to the Divine will, so he could also overcome his kind
nature in fulfillment of the Divine will. To do otherwise is simply to be
led by one's own nature.

Many people fail to grasp this point. They feel that kindness is
always warranted, and cruelty never is. A student once told me that she
had attended a Rosh Hashanah (Hebrew new year) service in a Reform
Temple in Cherry Hill, New Jersey. The reading from the Torah that
day was the above story of Abraham almost sacrificing Isaac. God
stopped him at the last moment. In an open discussion of this episode
both the rabbi and congregants were very critical of Abraham. They
felt that no one should ever kill anyone else, even if God commands it.

A decade and a half later that Reform rabbi was arrested and
eventually convicted for murdering his wife. Apparently he had a
paramour, and he hired someone to kill his own wife, the mother of his
children. This is relative morality in action. This man "felt" it was wrong
for Abraham to sacrifice Isaac, and he "felt" it was right for him to
eliminate his wife, who got in the way of his pleasure. If he had listened
to God, he would have had it the other way around.

Another common misconception is that education engenders
morality. People tend to think of highly educated, intellectual people
as models of lofty morality. That this is patently false was proven by
the Holocaust.

Germany was the pinnacle of scientific, cultural, and philosophical
development in all of Europe, but that did not stop it from wantonly
murdering millions of innocent people in the most sadistic ways.
Moreover, the book *Generation Des Unbedingten*[60], by Michael Wildt
of Hamburg University, chronicles that the SS forces, those who ran
the concentration camps, were comprised of some of the most educated
people in German society. The elite of intellectuals and academics, a
consortium of Ph.D.s in literature, philosophy, law, history, and science,
directed the genocide.

---

[60]   Loosely translated as "A Generation of True Believers," a 950 page work
       published in Germany

A famous story is told about Bertrand Russell while he was Professor of Ethics at Harvard. Russell was engaged in eyebrow-raising sexual antics that were highly unacceptable in Boston in the early 20th century. The Dean summoned him and excoriated him for his behavior, especially irate that a Professor of Ethics should be acting so unethically. Russell rejoined: "I was a Professor of Geometry at Cambridge, but no one ever expected me to be a triangle or a square."

Bertrand Russell, one of the leading philosophers of the 20th century and the winner of the Nobel Prize in Literature, was maintaining that what a person studies and teaches need have no bearing on his behavior. This is the polar opposite of the Torah viewpoint. According to Torah, what one studies and teaches must become an integral part of his or her life.

The objective of Torah study is to form a Torah-ingrained personality. Education has always been a prime value in Judaism not for the sake of intellectual proficiency, but as a means of passing on Torah values and proper behavior.

That's why, while Europe was languishing from illiteracy, trivial sparring, and wanton bloodshed, the Jews put their greatest value on learning as the conduit for morality. As Paul Johnson writes:

> In the darkest ignorance of the Dark Ages, study was regarded by the Jews as a religious duty second to none . . . To the Jews of the Middle Ages, the highest ambition and ideal was—not to be rich, but to be counted among the learned in the community. Ignorance was a disgrace, for it was only the scholar who commanded true respect . . . The sharpening of the mind by the dialectics and arguments in which the Talmud, the chief object of Jewish study, abounds, produced a zest for knowledge. . .[61]

> Far from feeling degraded the medieval Jews certainly considered themselves superior to their surroundings . . . they represented a moral standard which eschewed the bloodshed and inhuman cruelties that tainted their neighbors; they upheld

---

[61]   *The History of the Jews* (E.P. Dutton and Company, London, 1953) pp. 105-106

a pure and affectionate family life which won over the unwilling admiration of their enemies; they formed a voluntary brotherhood which knew of no serf or slave; they represented a culture of acknowledged grandeur which reached back a thousand years before their adversaries were heard of; in an age when many of the highest dignitaries and even princes could hardly write their names, the Jews employed a system of universal education . . . The Jew was a sober, industrious and sexually moral man in his daily affairs.[62]

The reason why Jews, unlike their gentile neighbors, never perpetrated atrocities and always eschewed violence is because they followed the instruction book on being human. They not only studied the Torah, but also lived it. King Solomon summed up this entire thesis in the end of Ecclesiastes: "The end of the matter, all having been heard: Fear God and keep his commandments; for that is what makes a human being."

---

[62]   ibid. pp. 106-107

Nine

7 Laws

A UFO lands near your house. Three green aliens emerge from the UFO portal. One alien holds in his hand a precious document that dazzles in beauty and brilliance. Without communicating with you, he entrusts you with this artifact. He then retreats into his UFO and takes off, back into space.

You are stupefied! An extraterrestrial creature has just handed you a document! After recovering from your initial shock, you immediately contact NASA. It is determined that the document is genuine—and priceless. Scholars the world over are engaged in order to decipher the extraterrestrial message contained in the document. Even when the language code is broken, most of the words are cryptic. Some passages even seem foolish. However, all the scholars agree that this document has inestimable value because of its source—beings from a different solar system.

How much more valuable would be a document that came not from another solar system, but from another dimension entirely? How valuable would be a document that came from the infinite God Himself?

This is the origin of the Torah. An entire nation witnessed a direct revelation of the Divine that left as its artifact the Ten Commandments and subsequently the remainder of the written Torah. No wonder that scholars throughout history have pored over its every word and letter! The sages refer to the Torah as essentially "black fire on white fire." This chapter will prove that the document of ink on parchment known as the Torah is a corporeal rendering of a staggering cosmic revelation.

The Seven Laws for All Humankind

Had Adam been worthy, then all his children—all of humankind— would have been The Chosen People. This, indeed, was God's original plan. He created a human being who would be the highest form of creation and capable of accepting His goodness. God also created a means through which man would receive this good: the Torah, God's blueprint for creation.

Because of Adam's sin, however, the Torah was restricted to the small portion of mankind who would be worthy of receiving it. The rest of humanity was given seven commandments, binding on every human being:

1. Not to worship idols
2. Not to blaspheme God
3. To establish courts of justice
4. Not to murder
5. Not to commit illicit sexual relations
6. Not to steal
7. Not to eat flesh from a living animal

Although known as the "Seven Laws of Noah," six of these commandments were given to Adam after the sin. The seventh was given to Noah, because it was in his time that God permitted the consumption of animals.

These are principle or primary commandments of which there are many derivations, extensions, and secondary laws. For example, the prohibitions against idolatry and blasphemy taught man to worship and respect God, this being the foundation of all morality and ethics. This was further strengthened by the commandments forbidding murder, incest/adultery, and robbery, as well as the one requiring social justice. Maimonides[63] writes in his *Guide to the Perplexed* that the prohibition against eating flesh from a living animal separated man from the savage, teaching him respect for other living creatures and control of his base appetite.

Ten generations passed from Adam until Noah. These were years of spiritual desolation, fraught with social dissidence and wanton ignorance of these special laws. Only Noah observed these laws and was described by the Bible as "a righteous person, perfect in his generation." Noah, however, was unable to sway and inspire the people of his generation and to perpetuate this ideal within his own family. He failed to achieve the desired result of forming a nation capable of receiving the Torah.

Chosen to Receive the Torah

Another ten generations passed before Abraham was born. Abraham became the progenitor of the Jewish nation. Abraham's grandson Jacob fathered the twelve tribes, each of whom adhered to this first monotheistic religion. At last, God had found potential recipients for His Torah. At last, "the chosen nation" was in the making.

Being "chosen", is a huge responsibility. It is not supposed to engender haughtiness or excessive pride. On the contrary, it is supposed to lead the "chosen people" to make every inhabitant of the world feel chosen and special. The "chosen people" are supposed to be a "light unto the nations."

The Torah is God's own instruction manual for planet Earth, given to the Israelites in an unprecedented act of revelation to an entire nation. Judaism is the religion based upon the Torah and its commentaries. As Samson Rafael Hirsch elaborates: [64]

> Jewish law is the only system of laws that did not emanate from
> the people whose constitution it was intended to be. Judaism is
> the only religion that did not originate from human beings who

---

[63] (1135-1204) The greatest medieval rabbi-philosopher and physician. He served as physician to the Sultan of Egypt.

[64] (1808-1888), the great rabbi, philosopher and builder of German Judaism

find in it the spiritual basis for their lives. It is precisely this objective quality of the Jewish law and religion that makes them both unique, setting them apart clearly and explicitly from all else on earth that goes by the name law or religion. It makes Jewish law the sole cultural factor in mankind that may be considered the activator and culmination of every other manifestation of progress, while in itself, as the given absolute ideal, the Law remains above all manifestations of human progress. All other religions and codes of law have originated only in the human of a given era; they merely express the conceptions of God, of human destiny, and of their relationship to God and to one another held by a given society at a specified period in history. Hence all these man-made religions and codes, like all other aspects of human civilization—science, art and folkways—are subject to change with the passing of time. For by their very nature and origin they are nothing but expressions of levels reached by civilization at various stages in human development.

Not so Jewish religion and law. They do not stem from beliefs held by human beings at one period or another. They do not represent time-bound human concepts of God, of things human and divine. They are God given, they contain ideas that, by the will of God, should mold the concepts of men for all time with regard to God and to things Divine, but above all with regard to man and human affairs.[65]

The Bible itself bears witness to the great act of Divine revelation that revealed the Torah:[66]

For inquire now regarding the early days that preceded you, from the day when Hashem your God created man on the earth, and from one end of heaven to the other end of heaven: Has there ever been anything like this great thing or has anything like it been heard? Have a people ever heard the voice of God

---

[65]   In *The Pentateuch* (Judaica Press, New York, 1986) p. 279

[66]   Deuteronomy, 4:32

speaking from the midst of the fire, as you have heard, and survived? You have been shown in order to know that Hashem, He is God! There is none beside Him! From heaven he caused you to hear His voice in order to teach you, and on earth He showed you His great fire, and you heard His words from the midst of the fire, because He loved your forefathers, and he chose his offspring after Him, and took you out before Himself with His great strength from Egypt.

The major claim of Judaism, which must be validated, is that the Torah is God's Word. Although Moses wrote down the Torah, he was a mere stenographer. God dictated the Torah, in its entirety, to Moses. The logical inference from this claim is that the Torah is eternal and immutable. Can this claim be proven?

Prophecies and Physical Realities

The first piece of evidence that supports the Divine authorship of the Torah is its many promises and prophecies that, however improbable, have come true. For example, the miracle of the survival of the Jewish people was predicted in the Torah.[67] No human being could have guaranteed the eternal survival of a particular people. This prediction is all the more amazing because the same Torah prophesized that the Jewish people would be exiled from their land and scattered among the other nations, where they would be persecuted and remain "small in number." That any nation should manage to endure such conditions of exile and persecution and survive is, by all odds, extremely unlikely. Yet history has proven that both these contradictory predictions have been fulfilled.

Another prediction we have already written about is that the Jewish people would return to their ancestral homeland, a feat unprecedented in history and certainly against all odds.

Soviet historian Nicolas Berdyaev said of the Jewish people:

Their destiny is too imbued with the metaphysical to be

---

[67] Leviticus, 26:44

[68] *The Meaning of History* (Charles Scribner's Sons, New York, 1936)

explained in either material or positive-historical terms.[68]

He further wrote:

> I remember how the materialist interpretation of history, when I
> attempted in my youth to verify it by applying it to the destinies
> of peoples, broke down in the case of the Jews, where destiny
> seemed absolutely inexplicable from the materialistic standpoint.
> And, indeed, according to the materialistic and positivist
> criterion, this people ought long ago to have perished.[69]

Secular Corroboration

Ancient Egyptian hieroglyphics are in consonance with biblical
accounts of the plagues visited upon the Egyptians. For example the
Ipuwer Papyrus, a papyrus consisting of the words of an Egyptian
named Ipuwer, which was acquired in 1828 by the Leiden Museum in
the Netherlands, seems to verify the historicity of the Torah version.[70]
Archaeological expeditions led by renowned archaeologists like Sir
Charles Woolley, Yigal Yadin, Marcel Dieulify, Henrik Bruins, and
others, have turned up evidence that authenticates the biblical
narrative.[71]

The London-based *Nature* journal, recorded a recent excavation
(September 2003) that confirmed the accuracy of the Bible. It had been
reputed that Jerusalem's Siloam Tunnel is the tunnel of King Hezekiah

---

[69]   Ibid.

[70]   In 1909 the text, translated anew, was published by Alan H. Gardiner under
the title, *The Admonitions of an Egyptian Sage form a Hieratic Papyrus in
Leiden* and is quoted extensively by Professor Immanuel Velikovsky in *Ages
in Chaos* (Abacus Publishing, 1978)

[71]   For further corroborative research read, *Israel in Egypt: The Evidence for
Authenticity of the Exodus Tradition* (James K. Hoffmeier, Oxford University
Press, 1999), *Pharaohs and Kings: A Biblical Quest* (David Rohl, Random
House, 1996), and The Patriarchal Age—Myth or History? (Kenneth Kitchen,
Biblical Archaeological Review, March-April, 1996)

of Judea, as is stated in Kings II, Chapter 20. According to the Bible, the tunnel was built to protect the city's water supply against an imminent Assyrian siege. This was totally substantiated by geologists at Hebrew University.

G. Ernest Wright, famed archaeologist and president of the American Schools of Oriental Research, wrote:

> The biblical scholar no longer bothers to ask whether archaeology proves the Bible . . . such a question is certainly to be answered in the affirmative.[72]

As Professor John Bimson wrote, "The biblical traditions and the archaeological evidence relate with striking accuracy."[73]

According to famed archaeologist, Dr. W.F. Albright, who was Professor of Semitic Languages, Johns Hopkins University:

> The Mosaic tradition is so consistent, so well attested by different pentateuchal documents, and so congruent with our independent knowledge of the religious development of the Near East in the late second millennium B.C., that only hypercritical pseudo-rationalism can reject its essential historicity.[74]

---

[72] Cited in *Faith and Archeology*, Biblical Archeology Review (March/April 1993), p. 57

[73] *Redating the Exodus and Conquest* (Sheffield: The Almond Press, 1981), p. 215-216

[74] *Archaeology and the Religion of Israel*, Johns Hopkins University Press (Maryland, 1956), page 96

Ten

Secrets of the
Universe

The Bible began with the Five Books of Moses and was supplemented by the Books of the Prophets. Until the early period of the second Temple, various prophets enunciated guidance on morals and values, and prophesized what should be expected in the future. Although there were thousands of prophets, only the prophecies and messages of fifteen prophets were included in Scripture, because only these would command eternal relevance. The Five Books of Moses, the Books of the Prophets, and the Writings (such as Psalms, Proverbs, and The Book of Ruth) are referred to as "the Written Law."

But there is much more to the Torah—a whole body of knowledge that was not recorded until world events made it necessary to consign them to writing for fear of losing them altogether. This is called "the Oral Law."

The Written Law is only a template—an ambiguous manual. The bulk of Torah knowledge was transmitted orally from Sinai through the generations. This consisted of practical, applied explanations of the Written Law that were committed to memory. For 1400 years it was forbidden to write down the Oral Law.

The Law had to become part and parcel of their fiber and beings. Something that is written down can be used as a crutch. One can always say, "I will refer to the text, instead of internalizing it." This would inhibit the people from knowing and living the law fluently.

The Romans governed the Jews during and after the Second Temple period. Sometimes the Romans prohibited the study of Torah and at other times they made conditions so difficult that the study of Torah was impossible except for the most courageous and hardy. Thus, during the Roman period a dispensation was granted to record the Oral Law. This body of literature is known as the Talmud.

Whereas the Written Law was general and cryptic, the Oral Law was the comprehensive guide that deciphered every ambiguity. The Oral Law is as holy as the Written Law. Without the Oral Law, the Written Law could not be practiced.

For example, the Torah[75] commands the Jews to wear an item called *tefillin*. The commandment is extremely vague. What are *tefillin*? Where should one put them on? How should one put them on? When should they be put on? Who should put them on?

The Written Law is terse and ambiguous. Yet we find that, although the Written Torah does not provide any explanatory details about *tefillin*, the Jewish people (who are not known for their harmonious agreement with each other) unanimously agree on the particulars of *tefillin*. Every pair of *tefillin* is black, square, made of leather, placed on the muscle of the forearm as well as the head, and not worn on the Sabbath or holidays. No Jew has ever presumed to suggest that *tefillin* should be round or hexagonal, brown or purple. How do Jews know all these details? Only from the Oral Law. At the same time God gave the commandment of *tefillin* in the written Torah, He explained its details in the oral Torah.

Another example: In Deuteronomy 12:21, God gives the command to ritually slaughter an animal. God states: "You must slaughter animals as I have commanded you." But where did He already command it? The Written Torah provides no details whatsoever about kosher slaughter, such as where on the animal's body it should be slaughtered, or whether it can be done slowly, or whether the knife used must meet any requirements.

---

[75]   Exodus 13:16

Obviously, the Written Law was not the only Law that God gave. An auxiliary Law must have also been given, one that defined, instructed, and provided details. In fact, the laws of kosher slaughter spelled out in the Talmud stipulate that the animal must be slaughtered with one swift cut of the esophagus and trachea, and that the knife used must be checked to be razor-sharp and free of any nicks that would cause unnecessary pain to the animal being slaughtered.

The Talmud

The Oral Law was first codified in the Mishna (188 C.E.) and later in the Gemara (500 C.E.) Together the two books (comprising more than thirty-six thick volumes) constitute the Talmud. The Oral Law is also comprised of the Midrash and Kabbalah.

The Talmud expounds on every area of Biblical legislation: all Jewish rituals from the cradle to the grave, financial obligations, torts, damages, social responsibility, and many other significant topics. An article in the prestigious "New York University Law Review" describes the Talmud:[76]

> The U.S. constitution contains a little over 5,000 words; the Talmud is over 5,000 pages long. What one fundamental legal document accomplishes through generality and stark simplicity,

---

[76] By Professors Irene Merker Rosenberg and Yale L. Rosenberg, New York University Law Review, Volume 63, Number 5, November 1988. The Journal in introducing the article writes, "For Professors Rosenberg, the American privilege against self-incrimination, as exemplified in Miranda v. Arizona, is a timid and ineffectual doctrine at best, failing to offer consistent protection to suspects from whom a confession of guilt is sought. Professors Rosenberg contrast the American approach with an ancient and far more unitary doctrine; the rule in Talmudic law that barred confessions in almost all criminal and quasi-criminal cases, whether by defendant or witness, in court or out-of-court, voluntary or coerced . . . They decline to propose that the United States adopt the ancient Talmudic rule, however. Instead, the authors illustrate more generally the benefits to be gained from comparative study, and in particular, the study of the complex masterpiece, the Talmud."

the other does through specificity and rich detail, making each in its own way a compact for the ages . . .

> Taking as their springboard the casuistic hornbook law of the Mishna, the Talmud scholars argued, extrapolated, and attempted to reach conclusions on legal issues of every conceivable kind. But it is the debates themselves, rather than the rules propounded, that are the glory of the Talmud. In the far ranging discussions of the Sages, no question is too hypothetical, no subject is deemed irrelevant or taboo. Profound conceptualization and logic are found alongside mysticism and stories, and free, though not random, association of legal subjects and concepts is the norm.

Some readers may think that the Talmud is outdated, because, for example, it discusses damages in terms of an ox goring another ox, not a car hitting another car. In truth, the Talmud is a book of principles that can be applied in any time and circumstance. It speaks in the language of ancient Judea, but its rulings are applied by learned rabbinic scholars to the most modern problems and occurrences.

Another point of confusion for people who take a superficial peek into the Talmud are fantastic narratives that seem like they could never be true. In an overview to the love ode *Song of Songs*, a masterful writer explains such passages:

> During the mid-nineteenth century period of the most vicious czarist persecutions of Jews, it was common for the leading rabbis to visit St. Petersburg to plead the case of their people with the czar's ministers. During one of these visits, a Russian official asked a visitor how he could account for the many tales in the Talmud, which were patently "inconceivable." The rabbi answered, "You know very well that the Czar and his advisors have often planned to promulgate decrees that would order the expulsion of the entire Jewish population. If God had not had mercy on us and thwarted your plans, the decree would have been written and placed before the Czar for his signature. He

would have dipped his pen into the inkwell and signed. His
signature would have made final the greatest Jewish catastrophe
in centuries. A poet might write that a drop of ink had swept
away three million people. All of us would have understood
what he meant. But a hundred years later, someone might read
this and consider it nonsense. In truth, the expression is apt and
pithy; it is only a lack of knowledge that could lead a reader to
dismiss it out of hand."

So it is with many parables of our Sages. They were written in the
form of a far-fetched story to conceal their meaning from those who
were unqualified to understand. None of us are qualified, so we laugh
at the stories instead of lamenting our puny stature. In general history
as well, many figures of speech have an obvious meaning to those
familiar with them, but are incomprehensible to the uninitiated. Everyone
knows that a shot cannot be heard more than several hundred yards
away. But every American knows that "the shot heard round the world"
began the American Revolution.[77]

Talmud for the 21ˢᵗ Century

In the book of Ecclesiastes, King Solomon, the wisest of all men,
wrote, "There is nothing new under the sun." He meant that all
developments—be they in technology, science, medicine, agriculture,
or other fields—all existed since the beginning of time. This is true
because God's Torah was the blueprint of creation. According to the
Zohar (the authoritative text on mysticism):

> God looked into His Law and created the world. Everything in
> the world is a mere reflection and personification of what is
> contained in the Divine blueprint. In a standard blueprint, the
> building can survive the loss or wear and tear of the blueprint.
> The Torah is not a standard blueprint. The world thrives and is

---

[77]   By R. Nosson Sherman in Overview to *Song of Songs* (Mesorah Publications,
New York, 1986)

sustained only on account of Torah. If the Torah would become lost, the world would revert to nothingness.

Another book on Kabbalah states:

> The principle is that everything that was, is, and will be—all of this is encapsulated in the Five Books of Moses. And not only general facts, but every minute detail, everything that will occur, all is hinted to in the Bible.[78]

The objective of the scholars of the Talmud was to delve into the inner-workings of the Divine blueprint. Often the Talmud goes off on a tangent that reveals the futuristic knowledge of these great sages. For example, the Talmud contains discussions about such "hot" medical topics as liposuction, surrogate pregnancy, and organ transplants.

On a very deep level, the Torah contains all the secrets of the universe. Here is but one example of the genius of the Oral Law: The Talmud[79] points out that the intestines of a pig are almost identical to that of a human. In Talmudic times, a plague struck that killed myriads of pigs. The rabbis proclaimed that a fast be observed amongst the people. They feared that the illness that was ravaging the pigs would affect the human population. The basis for the suspicion of possible disease was not because of the people eating pork; Jews are prohibited from eating pork. The reason was because of the anatomical similarity that pigs share with humans, namely the absence of a rumen. Due to the rabbis' knowledge and foresight, the people were saved from what would have been a disastrous outcome.

In 1918, the influenza pandemic, otherwise known as the Spanish Flu, ravaged the world. This global disaster claimed between 20-40 million lives in one year. "La Grippe" killed more people than the Great War, which lasted from 1914 to 1918 and killed 9 million men. By the time the pandemic ended in 1919, it had killed an estimated 50 million people. It was not until 1997

---

[78] Rabbi Elijah, known as The Genius of Vilna (1720-1797) in his commentary to the *Book of Concealment*

[79] Quoted from the Jerusalem Talmud in Tosafot, Talmud Taanis 21b

that the lungs of an eighteen-year-old soldier, Roscoe Vaughan, killed by the disease in September 1918, were used to obtain the genetic code of the disease. It was discovered that the disease started as a virus passed from birds to pigs. The pig immune system had forced the virus to mutate in order to survive, and it then infected humans. Only after so many had died did science realize the connection that exists between pigs and humans—a fact that the rabbis recorded so many centuries before.

Dr. Louis Pasteur is credited with the discovery of antibodies, vaccinations, and immunizations. Contemporaries and intimates of Pasteur write[80] that he garnered his knowledge from a French translation of the Talmud. The Talmud, in a section concerning different legal technicalities of healing an ill patient,[81] speaks about vaccination for a victim of rabies.

Electricity too is not a recent discovery. Although Benjamin Franklin is credited for having discovered electricity, the Talmud, in discussing the laws of Sabbath, already recorded such a discovery.[82] It was the practice of the pagan Emorites to install a rod in different places for purposes of a good omen. The Talmud determined that if one's intention in placing a rod in a place where chickens are present is to ward off the effects of lightning, it is permissible because the rod will conduct the lightening and protect the chickens.

Almost two thousand years ago, the scholars of the Talmud[83] broached a question that perplexes modern science and criminologists today:

> Is criminality genetically or physiologically linked? A woman was condemned by the government to be burned at the stake. After she was burned, the students of Rabbi Yishmael, who himself was a physician of note, collected her bones to discover the reasons for her criminality. This autopsy showed that the body had a number of defects. One of the defects listed was that the woman had 252 bones: four more than the average person.

---

[80]   *Mavoh Shearim* by R. Dr. I. M. Rabinowitz of Paris who translated the Talmud

[81]   Talmud, Yoma 84a

[82]   Tosefta, Shabbos 7:10

[83]   Talmud, Bechoros 45a

According to recent studies, more than half of all Americans are afflicted with obesity. Modern research shows that overweight people face the danger of a whole range of diseases. Liposuction is a modern technique used to remove excess fat from the body. The Talmud[84] records that a certain Rabbi Elazar, who was very obese, underwent a surgical operation under the influence of a "sleep medicine" in order to have his weight reduced. The surgeons (also rabbis) removed pounds of fat, and the operation was a success.

The Talmud also describes a neurosurgical operation to remove a foreign presence in the brain.[85] The patient was given an anesthetic drug and placed in a sterile room. The Talmud elaborates that a mixture of herbs was boiled together and poured upon the patient's head until his skull became soft allowing it to be cut open and the particle removed. It is mind-boggling to consider that the the sages had a drug capable of removing a foreign body and even more astounding that they were able to locate where the brain tumor was situated without the benefit of MRIs.

NASA scientists discovered the precise time that it takes for the moon to make a complete lunar rotation, as well as when the lunar cycle begins and ends. In their effort to calculate these complex details, they spent vast sums of money and used satellites to record information. Yet this precise information was already known thousands of years earlier without any satellites or computers. The Talmud[86] quotes a Torah tradition, dating back to Moses at Sinai, that the lunar cycle is 29 days, 12 hours, 44 minutes, and 3 1/3 seconds. According to the Talmud, the lunar cycle is 29.53059 days. NASA, after three years of research, calculated the number to be 29.530588 days.

For hundreds of years astronomers were under the mistaken impression that the star cluster known as the Pleiades consisted of no more than eight stars. Finally, beginning in the year 1609, with the advent of telescopes and (later) radio telescopes, astronomers realized that the Pleiades encompassed well over one hundred stars. The

---

[84]   Talmud, Baba Metzia 83b

[85]   Talmud, Kesuvos, 77b

[86]   Talmud, Rosh Hashana 25a

Talmud[87] 2,000 years ago noted the oral tradition from Sinai that the Pleiades is composed of over one hundred stars.

The Talmud, without benefit of any sophisticated astronomical devices, recorded the tradition, handed down from Moses at Sinai, that the number of stars in the universe totals approximately 1.0643×10^{18}. Contemporary astronomers approximate that there are 100 billion stars in our galaxy and 100 billion galaxies in our universe. Thus, there are approximately 100 billion times one hundred billion stars, or approximately 1.0×10^{21}.

Fifteen hundred years before the British astronomer Edmund Halley (1656-1742), Rabbi Joshua mentions the comet that would later become known as Haley's Comet.[88] According to the Talmud, Rabbi Joshua Ben Chanania, one of the great Talmudic personalities, was on a maritime voyage. He commented to Rabbi Gamliel that the trip was fraught with danger because there is a star that appears approximately once in seventy years that would lead the captain to confusion. While certain modern commentators dispute whether Rabbi Joshua's "star" was Haley's comet, since one of the periodic returns of Halley's comet was in the year 66, whereas the journey of Rabbi Gamliel to Rome was in the year 95, it is nevertheless remarkable that the periodic time of at least one comet was known to Rabbi Joshua in the second century. Interestingly, Haley was adamant that this discovery be recorded in the annals of history as an English discovery.

An interesting case of Talmudic jurisprudence being utilized in a contemporary situation took place in 1977. Siamese twins joined at the chest were born to a young Jewish couple. Only one heartbeat was audible. Examinations revealed that one baby had a four-chambered heart and the other baby a two-chambered heart, with only a very narrow wall separating the two hearts. Since one and a half hearts are not enough to sustain two lives, the parents and doctors were in a quandary. There was a possibility that through severing the twins, the twin with the four-chambered heart might live, however, the other twin would die. Would it be moral to kill one twin so that the other one might live?

---

[87]   Talmud, Berachos 58b

[88]   Talmud, Horyos 10a

This question was brought to Rabbi Moshe Feinstein (1894-1986), the world's leading decider of Jewish law. After much investigation into the relevant Talmudic principles, as well as medical consultation with the chief surgeon at the Children's Hospital in Philadelphia, Rabbi Feinstein reached a conclusion. He declared that within the framework of Jewish Law, it was permissible to operate on the twins so that one of them might live, even though it meant certain death for the other twin. This excruciating decision was based on the Talmudic dictum that a person or creature lacking a functioning heart is considered to be legally dead. Since one baby was already designated for death, the operation could proceed. The State Court of Pennsylvania, to which the attending doctors had applied, ruled similarly, showing that the wisdom of the Talmud never becomes obsolete.

Henceforth, we will refer to the Oral and Written Laws as the Torah.

Human
Sexuality

Eleven

The Super Bowl Halftime

F or the first time in history, the half-time show of the 2004 Super Bowl attracted more attention than the Super Bowl itself. In the middle of a duet sung by Justin Timberlake and Janet Jackson, Timberlake reached across Jackson's leather gladiator outfit and pulled off the sun-shaped, metal nipple decoration that was covering her right breast. More than 89 million Americans witnessed explicit "mature audience only" material on prime time T.V. The public response was outrage.

But what if the two celebrity performers had stuck to their script? Would there have been uproar? Presumably not. The apologies offered afterward were for deviating from the pre-rehearsed program. What was the program supposed to be? The two singers were performing a flirtatious duet, with Timberlake singing, "Rock Your Body." The lines he sang at the moment of truth were: "I'm gonna have you naked by the end of this song." So why all the outrage? The performer didn't want to pay lip service; he wanted to match word and deed. He wanted to take his art to the next level. If the song itself was not considered pornographic for prime time T.V., why was its acting out so scandalous?

What kind of society doesn't object to such lyrics? What kind of culture labels such a song, "art"? What kind of nation exalts as icons and role models performers who perpetrate such obscenity? Why is it acceptable for millions of American children to hear an idolized singer croon that he will have the woman next to him naked by the end of the song? Is that what we aspire to? Is that our objective—to get people naked?

Apparently so. The nude industry, a.k.a. the "Adults Only" industry, is one of the most lucrative industries in America. As a matter of fact, the most viewed website in the history of the Internet is—guess what— the video clip showing the baring of Janet Jackson's breast.

Ironically, the words "mature adult" at one time were used to describe a state of responsibility, development, adjustment, growth, and depth. Now the term "mature adult" conjures up images of pornography and perverted pleasure. "Mature adults" rent more than 800 million "adult" movies a year. There are 4.2 million pornographic websites—that's 12 percent of all websites in the world, totaling 372 million pornographic pages. Pornographic search engine hits total 68 million per day.

On Sunday, November 23, 2003, *Sixty Minutes* reported that some of America's largest corporations, such as General Motors, are involved in financing "adult" material. At hotels like the Marriott, Hilton, Hyatt, and Sheraton, "adult" in-house material accounts for more than 50% of generated profit. *Sixty Minutes* claims that 70% of hotel guests request such entertainment. Of all the cable networks, ESPN, CNN, Discovery, etc., the porn channel rakes in the most money. In all, the U.S "adult" industry is worth 12 billion dollars.

Our consternation at this situation begs the question: What's wrong with "Adult-Only" material? After all, people are free to engage in whatever gives them pleasure as long as it doesn't hurt others. But what if society itself is the victim?

"Adult entertainment" affects America's sexual mores. The "entertainment" does not stay on the computer or video screen, and those affected are not only adults. The youthful epidemic of "hooking up"— widespread, casual recreational sex, often with multiple partners—has been traced to the effect of television and Internet. Middle and high school children are experimenting with sex in the bathroom stalls at school, behind the gym, and in the back of the school bus. More children, at earlier ages, are engaging in sexual acts than ever before.

Sexual slavery is no longer confined to the Far East, Australia and other exotic locales. Statistics vary widely, but somewhere between 20,000 to 50,000 women and children are trafficked each year into the United States, primarily from Latin America, countries of the former Soviet Union and Southeast Asia, for exploitation in prostitution and the "sex industry."

Even child sexual abuse, rape and incest are slowly but surely gaining respectability. Currently, 100,000 websites offer illegal child pornography, and worldwide child porn generates $3 billion in revenues every year.

"Grand Theft Auto: Vice City" is America's number-one selling video game. The objective of the game is to commit grand larceny and engage in shooting sprees. The characters in the game appear almost nude. The game has served as the inspiration for teens to load themselves with rifles and conduct shooting rampages in their hometowns. The families of the victims have sued in court to make this game illegal.

Even more disconcerting and shocking than the game itself is the way it is marketed. The advertisement for "Grand Theft Auto: Vice City" proclaims: "It's not just a new frontier for games; it's a new frontier for humanity." Is this the direction in which humanity is moving?

Daily news reports are growing more and more frightening.

A recent news bulletin for a single day in July reported:[89]

Nineteen year old takes his martial arts sword and murders his sleeping father. . . . A man, his wife, and mother-in-law, found dead in the Gulf of Florida, an apparent murder-suicide. . . . Man arrested for putting insecticides on his girlfriend's lipstick and anti-depressant medication.

Here's a sampling of other recent news reports:

- Three teens in Camden, New Jersey were arrested with guns strapped to their backs and ammunition bulging in their pockets. They planned to drive around their hometown and exact revenge on enemies before traveling west. "There are 6 billion people on

---

[89]   July 18, 2002 - 1010 WINS NEWS

the Earth, and a few less wouldn't hurt," said alleged ringleader Matthew Lovett. Matthew, 18, and his sidekicks, Cody Jackson, 15, and Christopher Olson, 14, planned to kill three other teens in Oaklyn, drive around shooting randomly and then go to Missouri to "rescue" an online friend.[90]

- A ten-year old boy from New Jersey lured a three year-old boy from a library, sexually assaulted him, and then bludgeoned him to death.[91]
- Half of all young Americans will get a sexually transmitted disease by the age of 25. . . . The United States has the highest Sexually Transmitted Disease rate of any industrialized country, according to Center for Disease Control and World Health Organization.
- On February 10, 2005 a woman in Florida threw her newborn baby, less than one hour old, out the car window.

Sixty Minutes implied that the existence and growth of the Adult entertainment industry cause a licentiousness and moral breakdown. I think it is fair to say that we are in crisis. America is committing moral suicide.

In order to save America, we have to consider the pivotal question: What is the purpose of human existence? If the answer is "pleasure," then America's steep descent is at least on the right track. A different answer, however, could cause us to jump to a different track, leading in a totally different direction.

---

[90]   *New York Post,* August 27, 2003
[91]   As reported by CNN on March 28, 2003.

Getting High
on Ecstasy

❦

S peaking about a different track, a totally different direction . . .
Once five octogenarians were riding in a car, languidly
moving down the highway at 20 M.P.H. A state trooper pulled
them over, and asked them why they were going so slowly in a 70
M.P.H. zone. "Seventy-mile-an-hour zone?" the driver asked in
disbelief. "I distinctly saw a speed limit sign that said, '20'."

"That's the highway number, lady," the state trooper retorted. He
looked into the car and saw four other old ladies who looked ghastly
pale. "Why do your friends look so white?" he asked in concern.

The octogenarian driver answered, "Oh, we just got off of route 120!"

Sometimes in life it's easy to misread the signs. Most people, for
example, misread the "fun" or "pleasure" sign and think it means,
"happiness." As Dennis Prager so aptly wrote:

> I live in the land of Disney, Hollywood and year-round sun. You
> may think that people in such a glamorous fun-filled place are
> happier than others. If so, you have some mistaken ideas about
> the nature of happiness.

Many intelligent people will equate happiness with fun. The truth is that fun and happiness have little or nothing in common. Fun is what we experience during an act. Happiness is what we experience after an act. It is a deeper more abiding emotion.

Going to an amusement park or a ballgame, watching a movie or television, are fun activities that help us relax, temporarily forget our problems, and maybe even laugh. But, they do not bring happiness, because their positive effects end when the fun ends.

I have often thought that if Hollywood stars have a role to play, it is to teach us that happiness has nothing to do with fun. These rich, beautiful individuals have constant access to glamorous parties, fancy cars, expensive homes, everything that spells "happiness." But in memoir after memoir, celebrities reveal the unhappiness hidden beneath all their fun: depression, alcoholism, drug addiction, broken marriages, troubled children, profound loneliness.

Yet people continue to believe that the next, more glamorous party, more expensive car, more luxurious vacation, fancier home will do what all the other parties, cars, vacations, homes have not been able to do. The way people cling to the belief that a fun-filled, pain-free life equals happiness, actually diminishes their chances of ever attaining real happiness. If fun and pleasure are equated with happiness, then pain must be equated with unhappiness. But, in fact, the opposite is true: More times than not, things that lead to happiness involve some pain.

As a result, many people avoid the very endeavors that are the source of true happiness. They fear the pain inevitably brought by such things as marriage, raising children, professional achievement, religious commitment, civic or charitable work, self-improvement.

Human beings are born pleasure seekers. And what is the purpose of pleasure? To engender happiness, the true goal of most human striving.

Let us discuss pleasure seeking in Western culture. I think that most people would agree that "the pursuit of pleasure" for members of Western culture boils down to:

- The attainment of money and materialistic goods. This includes a luxury car, fashionable clothing, and an aesthetic dwelling place.
- Involvement in a relationship. In this pursuit, the aim is to seek a person who is as successful and attractive as possible.

Interestingly, many people who have succeeded in acquiring both these pleasures are neither happy nor fulfilled. Just a sampling of the lives of some of the greatest stars proves this point: Janis Joplin and Judy Garland died of an overdose. Marilyn Monroe killed herself. These stars had it all—money and romance, yet they were not happy.

In a paper entitled, "Does Economic Lot Improve the Human Lot?" famed economist Richard Easterlin showed that there is no real correlation between wealth and happiness. For classical economists, it was almost tautological to say that the wealthier people are, the happier they are too. Easterlin proved otherwise.

"Technology and Happiness," a study published in M.I.T.'s *Technology Review* (January, 2005) also revealed some surprising results. An axiom of Western culture is that people need money in order to buy the latest technological advances—state of the art computers, DVDs, sound systems, automobiles, etc. The implication is that possessing these items makes people happy. The M.I.T. study investigated Amish people, who, for reasons of religious principle, own no technologically advanced machines or gadgets. The report revealed that the Amish have depression rates that are negligibly lower than the rest of society's, while their happiness levels are consistently high.

A recent article in *Time Magazine* (January 17, 2005) makes the same point:

> So, what has science learned about what makes the human heart sing? More than one might imagine—along with some surprising things about what doesn't ring our inner chimes. Take wealth, for instance, and all the delightful things that money can buy. Research by Diener, among others, has shown that once your basic needs are met, additional income does little to raise your sense of satisfaction with life. A good education? Sorry, Mom and Dad, neither education nor, for that matter, a high IQ paves the road to happiness. Youth? No, again. In fact, older people are more consistently satisfied with their lives than the young. And they're less prone to dark moods: a recent survey by the Centers for Disease Control and Prevention found that people ages 20 to 24 are sad for an average of 3.4 days a month, as opposed to just 2.3 days for people ages 65 to 74. Marriage? A complicated picture: married people are generally happier than singles, but that may be because they were happier to begin with.

In the system I am about to present, you can enjoy pleasure and happiness all the time, regardless of your financial or social position. This system is dependent on you, on how you live your life. With the right structure and frame of mind, you can secure for yourself a continuous opportunity for pleasure and happiness.

The Secret of Happiness

People have discovered a wide variety of hyper-stimulating activities, addictions and desensitizers in order to substitute for what famous physician and author Dr. Deepak Chopra calls "the real thing." According to Chopra, alcohol, drugs and illicit sex are all material responses to a need that is not really physical at its foundation. It is because we have never learned to look for "the real thing", rather than mere sensation, it is hardly surprising that we don't find it.

Once a fisherman was sitting on his boat fishing. A much larger ship pulled up right along side him, and the captain engaged the fisherman in conversation. He asked the fisherman why he doesn't save up some money so that he can buy a larger boat and fish further from shore, securing for himself larger, more profitable fish. This way the fisherman could eventually buy an even larger boat and employ two or three hands, profit some more, and eventually purchase a ship and travel to distant places, catching exotic, expensive fish. Then the fisherman will be able to wholesale and amass a fortune of money. When the captain finally ended his proposition for the fisherman, the fisherman asked him, "And then what? After all those years of laborious work, what will I do after that?" The captain responded, "Well, *eventually* you will be able to retire and relax." The fisherman responded, "But I'm relaxing *now*."

According to the Torah, there is one major rule: *In order to be happy, in order to experience "the real thing", one has to appreciate life.* Life is the greatest blessing. A truly spiritual person always looks at what *he has*—the glass is always half full. He not only appreciates the little things in life, but also is *happy* because he has them. Every day of life is another opportunity for living, and living is joy. As the adage goes, "The happiest people don't necessarily have the best of everything; they just make the best of everything."

The *Time Magazine* article cited above offers the same key to happiness:

> At the University of California at Riverside, psychologist Sonja Lyubomirsky is using grant money from the National Institutes of Health to study different kinds of happiness boosters. One is the gratitude journal—a diary in which subjects write down things for which they are thankful. She has found that taking the time to conscientiously count their blessings once a week significantly increased subjects' overall satisfaction with life over a period of six weeks, whereas a control group that did not keep journals had no such gain.

Gratitude exercises can do more than lift one's mood. At the University of California at Davis, psychologist Robert Emmons found they improve physical health, raise energy levels and, for patients with neuromuscular disease, relieve pain and fatigue. "The ones who benefited most tended to elaborate more and have a wider span of things they're grateful for," he notes. . . .

Seligman has tested similar interventions in controlled trials at Penn and in huge experiments conducted over the Internet. The single most effective way to turbocharge your joy, he says, is to make a "gratitude visit." That means writing a testimonial thanking a teacher, pastor or grandparent—anyone to whom you owe a debt of gratitude—and then visiting that person to read him or her the letter of appreciation. "The remarkable thing," says Seligman, "is that people who do this just once are measurably happier and less depressed a month later. But it's gone by three months." Less powerful but more lasting, he says, is an exercise he calls three blessings—taking time each day to write down a trio of things that went well and why. "People are less depressed and happier three months later and six months later."[92]

Another key ingredient for happiness is altruism, doing something for others. Kirk Douglas realized this and wrote about it:

We are all born of royalty, within us is a tiny seed of Godliness—the spirit of God, the "Shechinah"—and throughout our life we must learn to nourish it. Obey the voice within—it commands us to give of ourselves and help others. As long as we have the capacity to give, we are still alive. It demands that even while you are hurting you realize that others are hurting too. When you stop giving, you die. To be able to give—not just money, but something of yourself to others, your love, your understanding—that is life itself.[93]

---

[92] *Time Magazine,* January 17, 2005

[93] In his book *Climbing the Mountain,* (Simon & Schuster, 2000)

This insight is corroborated by a study performed by researcher Sonja Lyubomirsky:

> Another happiness booster, say positive psychologists, is performing acts of altruism or kindness—visiting a nursing home, helping a friend's child with homework, mowing a neighbor's lawn, writing a letter to a grandparent. Doing five kind acts a week, especially all in a single day, gave a measurable boost to Lyubomirsky's subjects.

To be a Godly person one must realize the Godliness in others. This means recognizing that every creature, especially every person, is a creation of God. The Torah teaches that every person, no matter his religious, social, ethnic, or economic status, is created in the Divine image. Every human being is Divine and worthy of respect.

Structure

Now, appreciation and altruism may sound like a great program to live by, but there is one important prerequisite, and that is *structure*. In order to be happy a human being needs structure.

Without traffic laws, casualties and deaths would litter the highways. Nobody looks at traffic regulations as disadvantageous or non-pleasurable, because even a driver who might love to zoom his car beyond the speed limit appreciates that traffic regulations save lives. "Red lights" don't encroach on personal freedom; they keep the traffic flowing and prevent mayhem. They insure that everyone gets to his destination safely.

When seatbelts were first devised, most people opted not to wear them. They felt that seat belts were restrictive. Studies soon proved that seatbelts could save both drivers and passengers from serious injury and death. Now most people appreciate being held in by a seat belt.

Similarly, the Creator knew that in order for humans to be constantly happy, they needed structure and regulation. That's why God gave humans the Torah. Without such moral structure, human life would be mayhem.

Many people living in Western culture abhor the term "commandment," because they don't want to be commanded. This is why I call the 613 rules in the Torah "instructions." They are instructions on how to lead a more productive, healthy, happy, and rewarding life.

When M. Frederic Auguste Bartholdi, designer of the Statue of Liberty, sailed into New York Harbor, he said:

> We will rear here, before the eyes of the millions of strangers seeking a home in the New World, a colossal Statue of Liberty; in her up stretched hand the torch enlightening the world; in her other hand the Book of Laws, to remind them that true liberty is only found in obedience to law . . .

Or, as Plato said: "Freedom is the power to limit oneself."

One need only contemplate the total slavery of a person addicted to smoking to realize how illusory certain "freedoms" are. Or how about an obese person who is addicted to overeating? Would you call him free? An Internet junkie who can't avoid checking out the latest porn site is nothing but a slave. Is a workaholic free? What about a child who is so addicted to his video games that he seldom goes outdoors. Is he free?

In the words of a master educator:

> Ironically, for all of the talk of freedom, the concept is as sorely misunderstood as it is staunchly defended. Your average American will simply define freedom as the free reign to do as one pleases—with our more refined members adding the clause—as long as one doesn't hurt anybody. This is an obviously incomplete and distorted definition.
>
> The 60's were a testing ground for this type of freedom. Drugs and alcohol flowed freely; walls of modesty were dismantled; permissiveness in child rearing reigned. But did it bring about happiness and a sense of fulfillment? No! Is a drug addict who has open access to heroin a free man? Is a child allowed to run

wild better off than the child who has parents that do not allow such behavior? License to do whatever one wants, whenever one wants, makes him a slave to his base desires rather than securing liberty.

Paradoxically, freedom flourishes only through committing ourselves to a structure. Freedom requires form. One must have definitions of what is positive, decent, and moral; he must know what he wants. Only with principles and the fortitude to channel behavior to live by these truths can the benefits of freedom be reaped.[94]

Ultimate freedom comes when a person is in control of himself. In order to experience freedom, one has to have structure.

Interestingly, studies have proved that religious people tend to be happier:

On the positive side, religious faith seems to genuinely lift the spirit, though it's tough to tell whether it's the God part or the community aspect that does the heavy lifting. Friends? A giant yes. A 2002 study conducted at the University of Illinois by Diener and Seligman found that the most salient characteristics shared by the 10% of students with the highest levels of happiness and the fewest signs of depression were their strong ties to friends and family and commitment to spending time with them. "Word needs to be spread," concludes Diener. "It is important to work on social skills, close interpersonal ties and social support in order to be happy."[95]

Of course, from the standpoint of Torah, religious faith and close interpersonal ties to other people are not separate categories. The Torah mandates taking responsibility for one's fellow. In fact, the

---

[94]   R. Shlomo Freifeld (1920-1984), founding dean Shor Yoshuv Institute, Lawrence N.Y.

[95]   Time Magazine, Ibid.

commandment, "Love your neighbor as yourself," is defined by the classical commentators to include three specific actions:

- Treat your neighbor with honor.
- Help your neighbor with physical and financial assistance.
- Speak well of your neighbor.

By following such "instructions," as scientists have proved, one can achieve true happiness.

Thirteen

Sex and Violence:
the Causal Connection

... Which brings us back to that discreet transaction between
two people in private. If there's no evidence that it harms others,
then the state should let them get on with it. People should be
allowed to buy and sell whatever they like, including their own
bodies. Prostitution may be a grubby business, but it's not the
government's.

—*The Economist*, September 4, 2004

Just sixty years ago, a man without a shirt walking down a
metropolitan street could be arrested for "indecent exposure."
Today women are fighting for that right. Triple "X" video stores
and porn shops are rampant. There are no rules of modesty. Women
clothing items are cut so low that a popular comedian said, "Sometimes
in order to see what the woman is wearing you have to look under the
table." When *The Washington Post* reported last summer that fashions
for girls in the "teen" years were "long on skin, short on modesty," it
was noting a reality that many parents of teenagers know only too
well. A lot of what passes for pop culture at the moment seems

specifically oriented toward the gaze and delight of hormonally surging 17-year-old boys.

As reported by AOL News:

> "The 'whore wars' are a big issue," said Donna Cristen, who was shopping for back-to-school clothing on Thursday with her daughter, Tess, 13. Ms. Cristen's reference was to a term that arose on the Internet, where commentators like Betsy Hart of CNN complained that stores as mainstream as J. C. Penney, Target and the Limited Too were increasingly carrying clothing that could seem designed to suit the needs of women who work the Lincoln Tunnel on-ramp. "Dressing like a slut," Ms. Hart called it, and she was far from the first. Not long ago, the television commentator Bill Maher made the point that the way things are going in fashion, there will soon be nothing left for prostitutes to wear.

Even universities, supposedly dedicated to the pursuit of higher learning, are fraught with immorality. Harvard University, for example, is acknowledged as the number one university in the world. In February 2004, Harvard's deans announced that they would permit the publication of the first-ever Harvard student porn magazine. Camilla A. Hardy, one of the students behind the magazine said, "Initially there was some concern about the nudity aspect," but Harvard's Committee on College Life members (comprised of the administration and faculty of Harvard) eventually "got past the fear of porn."

In its 183-year history, the august Oxford Union debating society has heard the wisdom of British prime ministers and three U.S. presidents, including the likes of Winston Churchill, Ronald Reagan and other prominent figures such as Mother Teresa and the Dalai Lama. Now its members are to hear from porn star Ron Jeremy, star of 1,700 adult films. "Ron is the biggest and apparently the best in the business, so I'm sure he'll have some fascinating stories to tell," said Oxford Union librarian Vladimir Bermant, who organized the event. Jeremy, whose claim to fame is that he has slept with more than 4,000 women, addressed the union in March 2005.

Modesty and shame are on the fringe and pornography is in. The question is, so what? Obviously child porn is a severe form of child abuse and is exceedingly destructive. What about adult porn? Does this seemingly innocent, very pleasurable activity really cause any harm?

According to a Time Magazine Article (January 14, 2004) on the subject of porn and culture, porn has an adverse affect:

> In recent years, a number of psychologists and sociologists have joined the chorus of religious and political opponents in warning about the impact of pervasive pornography. They argue that porn is transforming sexuality and relationships—for the worse. Experts say men who frequently view porn may develop unrealistic expectations of women's appearance and behavior, have difficulty forming and sustaining relationships and feeling sexually satisfied. . . . Cyberporn is even giving rise to a new form of sexual compulsiveness. . . . "The Internet is the crack cocaine of sexual addiction," says Jennifer Schneider, co-author of *Cybersex Exposed: Simple Fantasy or Obsession?*

The vast majority of respondents—85% to 90%—according to Alvin Cooper, who heads the San Jose Marital and Sexuality Center, which conducted the study, are what he calls "recreational users," people who view pornography as a curiosity or diversion.

The question is, can even recreational use be unhealthy?

A 2003 online study by Texas Christian University found that the more pornography men watch, the more likely they are to describe women in sexualized terms and categorize women in traditional gender roles. Mark Schwartz, director of the Masters and Johnson clinic in St. Louis, Mo., says porn not only causes men to objectify women—seeing them as an assemblage of breasts, legs and buttocks—but also leads to a dependency on visual imagery for arousal. "Men become like computers, unable to be stimulated by the human beings beside them," he says. "The image of a lonely, isolated man masturbating to his computer is the Willy Loman metaphor of our decade."[96]

---

[96]   Time Magazine, Ibid.

What kind of impact does pornography have on an existing relationship?

> Sometimes pornography tears couples apart. At the 2003 meeting of the American Academy of Matrimonial Lawyers, two-thirds of the 350 divorce lawyers who attended said the Internet played a significant role in divorces in the past year, with excessive interest in online porn contributing to more than half of such cases. "This is clearly related to the Internet," says Richard Barry, president of the association. "Pornography had an almost nonexistent role in divorce just seven or eight years ago."[97]

There is also a religious reason to forbid pornography. The Torah severely proscribes recreational masturbation and deems somebody who intentionally wastes his seed as one who destroys creation.

Clothing

Is there a reason, according to evolutionists, why humans wear clothing? Why must we differ from other members of the animal world? That the world community at large, including societies that inhabit hot climates, wear some kind of clothing seems to suggest that, at least subconsciously, even atheists agree that there is something inherently unique about the human being.

Humans, unlike animals, have the moral sense to understand and protect their sexuality. As Aryeh Kaplan explains: "The main function of human clothing is to serve as a barrier against passion. Much evil would result if man's sexual passions were left unchecked, and in this respect, clothing provides protection from this evil."

Developments in modern American society have shown: the less clothes, the more promiscuity. I would like to suggest that the first step in reversing the moral breakdown of America is to return to a standard of modesty in dress.

---

[97]   Ibid.

Does Immorality Affect Society?

Dr. Francis Fukuyama, Professor of International Political Economy at Johns Hopkins University authored a fascinating article, *Human Order and the Reconstitution of Social Order*, which we will use as a template for our discussion. This article was subsequently published in his book, The Great Disruption: *Human Order and the Reconstitution of Social Order* (Free Press, 1999).

Professor Fukuyama analyzes and probes the root cause of the disintegration of social order and breakdown of morals that accompanied the spawn of the information age in the 1960's.

The West experienced a series of liberation movements that sought to free individuals from the constraints of traditional social norms and moral rules. The liberation sought by each of these movements concerned social rules, norms, and laws that unduly restricted the options and opportunities (usually sexual) of individuals. Pop psychology, from the human-potential movement of the 1960s to the self-esteem trend of the 1980s, sought to free individuals from stifling social expectations. America developed a culture of unbridled individualism, in which the breaking of rules becomes, in a sense, the only remaining rule.

Concomitantly, the mid-1960s were marked by seriously deteriorating social conditions in most of the industrialized world. Crime and social disorder began to rise. The dramatic rise in crime rate, in the mid 60's, was a striking departure from the early post-Second World War period, when U. S. murder and robbery rates actually declined. Marriages and births declined and divorce soared; and one out of every three children in the United States and more than half of all children in Scandinavia were born out of wedlock.

The Sexual Revolution destroyed our stock of shared values, therefore dissolving much of America's social connectedness. As Professor Fukuyama writes:

> True communities are bound together by the values, norms, and experiences their members share. The deeper and more strongly held those common values, the stronger the sense of community.

> A society dedicated to the constant spending of norms and rules in the name of expanding individual freedom of choice will find itself increasingly disorganized, atomized, isolated, and incapable of carrying out common goals and tasks . . . The same society that wants no limits on its technological innovation also sees no limits on many forms of personal behavior, and the consequence is a rise in crime, broken families, parents' failure to fulfill obligations to children, neighbors' refusal to take responsibility for one another, and citizens' opting out of public life.

Social scientists refer to a society's stock of shared values as "social capital." As Professor Fukuyama explains:

> Like physical capital (land, buildings, machines) and human capital (the skills and knowledge we carry around in our heads), social capital produces wealth and is therefore of economic value to a national economy . . . Social virtues such as honesty, reciprocity, and the keeping of commitments are not worthwhile just as ethical values; they also have a tangible dollar value and help the groups that practice them to achieve shared ends.

America was losing "social capital" and seemed to become the prototype for negative social capital in other developed countries.

- Divorce rates moved up sharply across the developed world; by the 1980s half of all American marriages could be expected to end in divorce, and the ratio of divorced to married people had increased fourfold in just thirty years.

- Births to unmarried women as a proportion of U.S. live-births climbed from under five percent to 32 percent from 1940 to 1995. The figure was close to 60 percent in many Scandinavian countries; the United Kingdom, Canada, and France reached levels comparable to that in the United States.

- The combined probabilities of single-parent births, divorce, and the dissolution of cohabiting relationships between parents (a situation common in Europe) meant that in most developed countries ever smaller minorities of children would reach the age of eighteen with both parents remaining in the household.

- The core reproductive function of the family was threatened as well: fertility has dropped so dramatically in Italy, Spain, and Germany that they stand to lose up to 30 percent of their populations each generation, absent new net immigration.

- Although the United States is exceptional among developed countries for its high crime rates, crime rose significantly in virtually all other non-Asian developed countries in approximately the same time period. Violent crime rose rapidly in Canada, Finland, Ireland, the Netherlands, New Zealand, Sweden, and the United Kingdom.

The fact that so many different social indicators moved across a wide group of industrialized countries concurrently, points us toward a more general level of explanation. As Professor Fukuyama points out:

> When the same phenomena occur in a broad range of countries,
> we can rule out explanations specific to a single country, such
> as the effects of the Vietnam War or of Watergate.

Several arguments have been put forward to explain why the phenomena we associate with the trend toward individualism occurred. It has been theorized that poverty and inequality were to blame.

The idea that such large changes in social norms could be brought on by poverty in countries that are wealthier than any others in human history is quite ludicrous. Professor Fukuyama notes that poor people in the United States have higher absolute standards of living than many Americans of past generations, and more per capita wealth than many people in contemporary Third World countries with more-intact family structures.

If poverty was to blame, then crime in Depression-era America should have been as rampant as it is today. The opposite was true; the Great Depression of the 1930s saw decreasing levels of violent crime in the United States. Also, there was no depression in the period from the 1960s to the 1990s to explain the sudden rise in crime; in fact, the great American postwar crime wave began in a period of full employment and general prosperity. Nor do we see any correlation between poverty and crime in Jerusalem, Israel's poorest city as assessed by level of per capita income. In fact, we see the opposite. In societies such as the Orthodox Jewish communities in Jerusalem and Bnei Brak (where the sexual revolution has had no impact), the crime rate remains low.

Professor Fukuyama suggests that the disintegration of social order and rise of crime and licentiousness can be attributed to a broad cultural shift that included the decline of religion and the promotion of individualistic self-gratification over community obligation. Increasing individualism and the loosening of communal controls clearly had a huge impact on family life, sexual behavior, and the willingness of people to obey the law.

How It Happened

Examining 19th century, as well as turn of the 20th century America, we find a country permeated by religious ideals and values. Family tradition, loyalty, and solidarity were more important than individual goals and romantic interest. The chief value of the Victorian-age family was RESPONSIBILITY. Relationships were based on "covenants"— virtually unbreakable commitments based on loyalty and responsibility.

The decline of Western morality can be traced to the inception of moral relativism, a concept we discussed and elucidated in previous chapters. Western rationalism began to undermine itself by concluding that no rational grounds supported universal norms of behavior. Friedrich Nietzsche, the father of modern relativism argued that man, the "beast with red cheeks," (an interesting rejoinder to Aristotle's "the rational animal") was a value-creating animal, and that the manifold "languages of good and evil" spoken by different human cultures were products of the will, rooted nowhere in truth or reason. Nietzsche's aphorism "There are no facts, only interpretations" became the watchword for later generations of relativists under the banners of deconstructionism and postmodernism.

This was followed by the founding of behavioral psychology by John Watson, who argued that tight social controls over behavior were not necessary for social order. Sigmund Freud contributed heavily to the corrosion of values, promulgating the idea that human emotional illness originated in the excessive social repression of sexual behavior. As Professor Fukuyama points out:

> Indeed, the spread of psychoanalysis accustomed an entire generation to talking about sex and seeing everyday psychological problems in terms of the libido and its repression.

Cultural historian James Lincoln Collier argues that the intellectual and cultural grounds for the sexual revolution of the 1960s had already been laid among American elites by the 1920s. Their spread through the rest of the population was delayed, however, by the Depression and the Second World War, which led people to concentrate more on economic survival and domesticity than on self-expression and self-gratification—which most, in any event, could not afford.

Sexual Immorality Equals Social Destruction

Dr. Fukuyama was born in 1952 and didn't write this particular dissertation until the 1990s. Yet the Nazis seemed to have been quite aware of the entire premise we have been discussing. When the Nazis conquered Poland in 1939, they flooded the bookstores with immoral material. They deliberately flooded Eastern Europe with pornography in order to destroy it culturally, politically and spiritually. One historian, Professor Ihor Kamenetzky describes the process this way:

> The German Propaganda Office . . . was supposed to organize or sponsor Polish burlesque shows and publish cheap literature, strongly erotic in nature . . . to keep the masses on a low level . . .

> These projects for degeneration and moral debasement were
> actually realized in the larger Polish cities . . . . [98]

Another historian writes about the Nazis:

> You know that the enemy is striving to destroy the Polish nation
> by demoralizing and degrading Polish youth . . . We are defeated
> whenever we see one of you entering a German movie or theater,
> reading a dirty book, or patronizing one of their gambling
> houses.[99]

The Germans perpetrated this method of indecency because they knew
that corroding the morals of the Poles would help the Nazi regime consolidate
its power and win the Poles' cooperation in its diabolical schemes.

I venture to hypothesize that the Nazis learned this lesson from the
Bible. The Bible describes the prelude to the Deluge that struck the
entire inhabited world, leaving as its sole survivors only Noah and his
family. What precipitated such a catastrophe? Why would God decide
that human society was beyond repair and needed to be replaced almost
in its entirety?

The Torah explains: "And the world was corrupted *(vatishaches)*"
with *"chamas." Chamas* means: violence, thievery, and murder. The
classical Biblical commentators ask what kind of corruption the word
"vatishaches" actually connotes. The gist of their question is what kind
of corruption could lead to such wickedness among people in a society.
They answer that *"vatishaches"* refers to sexual promiscuity and
immorality. In essence, they are saying that the society's pronounced
sexual immorality led to a corrupt society in which theft, murder, and
violence abounded.

This appears to be somewhat perplexing, because while both sexual
immorality and theft/murder are sins, they are certainly in different
categories. Sins of sexual immorality are for the most part "victimless

---

[98]   *Secret Nazi plans for Eastern Europe: A study of Lebensraum Policies* (College
and University Press, New Haven, Connecticut, 1961)

[99]   Jan Karski in *Story of a Secret State* (Boston: Houghton Mifflin Co., 1944), p.
307. See also p. 243.

crimes." Theft and murder, however, harm other people. Why should acts done in the bedroom affect the level of violence and theft in a society?

Here we learn a stark lesson. It is precisely the sins of a sexual nature that lead to a corrupt and pernicious society. When people indulge their sexual nature without boundaries, they are letting their bodies take control. Their only concern is their bodies' pleasure, and not how it may affect others. To satisfy their drives they will go to any lengths. Once they develop such sexual greed, they will attempt to acquire whatever they desire, no matter what it takes to do so. They will rob, cheat, murder, and rape, oblivious to the harm inflicted on others. The "victimless crime" invariably leads to a society rife with victims.

The Nazis understood the above principle all too well. This is why they flooded the bookstores of Poland with pornography immediately after their conquest. They knew that if they could encourage people to focus on their personal sexual needs, they would be more willing to cooperate with whatever immoral edicts the Nazis promulgated. The human reluctance to hurt other people is benumbed by sexual promiscuity.

This was consistent with the song sung by the "Hitler Youth": "We are the joyous Hitler Youth. We do not need any Christian virtue. Our leader is our savior. The Pope and Rabbi shall be gone. We want to be pagans once again."

Similarly, when the Bolsheviks took over Russia in 1917, sexual liberation was top on their agenda.

Yaron Svoray is an investigative journalist who went undercover to expose Germany's neo-Nazi movement. In his book, *In Hitler's Shadow*, he depicts today's neo-Nazis as men steeped in sexual immorality and pornography. In one episode, he records, neo-Nazis in their forties and fifties assembled together to watch a "surprise" movie of five American men sodomizing, raping, and torturing an eleven year old Mexican girl. He watched, stunned, as the neo-Nazis reveled and rejoiced and engaged in the basest acts of immorality while watching their "treat."

You Are What You Hear

On the other hand, a positive correlation does exist between rates of television viewing and sexual promiscuity and violent behavior.

In a study published in the September, 2004 issue of *Pediatrics*, researchers found that children who watched a lot of TV with sexual content were about twice as likely to start having intercourse during the subsequent year as those with little exposure to televised sex. Furthermore, according to behavioral scientist Dr. Rebecca Collins: "exposure to TV that included only talk about sex was associated with the same risks as exposure to TV that depicted sexual behavior."

From innuendoes to depictions of intercourse, sex is pervasive on TV and present in about two-thirds of all shows other than news and sports. Teens watch an average of three hours of television daily. According to the researchers, TV thus "may create the illusion that sex is more central to daily life than it truly is and may promote sexual initiation as a result."

Dr. Collins added that TV sex rarely deals with negative aspects most teens aren't prepared to deal with, including unwanted pregnancy, AIDS, and other sexually transmitted diseases. That "sends kids the message that everybody's having sex and nobody's thinking about responsibility and nothing bad ever happens," summarized Dr. Collins.

According to the Time article:[100]

> Porn doesn't just give men bad ideas; it can give kids the wrong idea at a formative age. . . . Older teens may be aware of the effects of such images: 59% of 15-to-24-year-olds told the pollsters they believe seeing porn on the Internet encourages young people to have sex before they are ready; 49% said it promotes bad attitudes toward women and encourages viewers to think unprotected sex is O.K. "Pornography is affecting people at an increasingly young age," says sociologist Diana Russell, who has written several books on the subject. "And unfortunately

---

[100]   January 14, 2004

for many kids growing up today, pornography is the only sex education they'll get."

. . . Recent studies show a correlation between increased aggressiveness in boys and exposure to pornography, and a link between childhood use of porn and sexually abusive behavior in adulthood.

Lawrence Kelemen, who devoted a chapter of his book on childrearing to the deleterious effects of television, summarizes how television engenders sexual promiscuity:

> Television watching also affects children's sexual behavior. Three studies presented at the annual meeting of the American Psychological Association demonstrated that the more television an adolescent viewed, the higher the probability that he/she would engage in sexual activity. Another study found the amount of television watched (especially MTV) to be the greatest predictor not only of sexual activity, but of the number of sexual partners a student would have. Hundreds of similar studies draw the same conclusion.[101]

Television watching also leads to violent and aggressive behavior and higher homicide rates. This was proved by a cross-cultural investigation conducted by Dr. Brandon Centerwall, professor of epidemiology at the University of Washington, Seattle. He discovered that before the introduction of television, the United States, Canada, and South Africa all had similar homicide rates. Ten to fifteen years after television was introduced in the United States and Canada, white homicide rates jumped by 92% and 93% respectively. (The time lapse allows the children who watch television to grow old enough to affect the homicide rate, since homicide is generally an adult activity.) Television arrived in South Africa almost thirty years after it was introduced in North America. Significantly, during the period when

---

[101] Lawrence Kelemen, *To Kindle a Soul* (Leviathan Press: 2001), p. 160

the North American white homicide rate spiked, the South African white homicide rate remained consistently low. Yet, the rate there followed the same pattern as North America, jumping 130% fourteen years after television was introduced.[102]

Lawrence Kelemen summarizes the evidence thus:

> There have been retrospective surveys, longitudinal studies, and meta-analyses. Tens of thousands of infants, children, teens, and young adults have been studied in every continent for their reactions to television, and the results have all produced the same conclusion. To date, more than a thousand investigations have documented a causal link between television viewing and violent behavior, and no study has contradicted this hypothesis.
>
> . . . The Surgeon General's 2001 report cited statistical links between television watching and violent behavior similar in strength to the evidence linking smoking and lung cancer. Dr. Jeffrey MacIntyre, legislative and federal affairs officer for the American Psychological Association, echoed these sentiments in an interview with the *New York Times:* "The evidence is overwhelming. To argue against it is like arguing against gravity."[103]

R. Shlomo Freifeld teaches a poignant lesson about listening to negative content:

> In the laws of personal injury, the Talmud sets a scale for how much must be paid for damaging different parts of the body. The sages say that if one should cause someone to become deaf, he must pay him the same amount as if he had killed him. For blinding a person, he must pay the value of the eye alone. For

---

[102]   Brandon S. Centerwall, "Television and Violence: The Scale of the Problem and Where to Go from Here." *Journal of the American Medical Association* 267, no. 22 (1992): 3059-61.

[103]   Lawrence Kelemen, *To Kindle a Soul,* pp. 167-168.

taking away the ability to hear, however, he must pay his entire value (Talmud, Baba Kama 85b).

The reason is that the ear is our primary receptacle for wisdom. Growth and change come from being able to hear a new insight. If one has his ears open and is receptive to new ideas, he can grow. If he closes his ears or is unable to hear, then he will remain the same. If we take away a person's ability to hear, we have severely limited his ability to grow. We have, in essence cut him off from his humanity. For this, he must pay him his entire value.

This uniqueness of hearing is even evident from our physical makeup. Of all our sensory organs, our ears are distinctive. All of our other senses work in both directions. Our eyes take in light and they let out tears. Our mouth takes in food and let out words. Only our ears work solely in one direction. They are receptors. They take in information, wisdom.

Nonviolent, wholesome children come from homes that scrutinize and monitor their children's entertainment. Every educator and parent must remember: "A child's mind is like wet cement—any impression lasts forever."

Fourteen

Cosmogony

The pagans used sex to explain the origins of the universe. Ancient cosmogonies (cosmogony refers to theories explaining the origin and creation of the world), whether it is the Babylonians, the Phoenicians, the Egyptians, the Hindus, the Greek, or the Romans, all describe their gods engaging in raucous and grotesque sexual relationships.

It is for this reason that religions themselves were inundated with sexual activity. Carnality was paramount in the religions of the ancient world. As recent as the last century Sri Lanka Buddhist worship of the goddess Pattini involved priests engaging in transvestitism and in general immoral, distorted sexual practices. Until it was made illegal in 1948, when India gained independence, Hindu temples in many parts of India had both women and boy prostitutes. In the fourteenth century, the Chinese found homosexual Tibetan religious rites practiced at the court of a Mongol emperor.

Sexualized cosmogony broke from the true ancient, primordial tradition—the Torah. The Torah has done more to civilize the world than any other book or idea in history. It is the Torah that gave humanity such ideas as a universal, moral, loving God; ethical obligations to this God; the need for history to move forward to moral and spiritual redemption; the belief that history has meaning; the notion that human freedom and social justice are the divinely desired states for all people and the concept of sexual holiness (the goal of raising human beings from the animal-like to the God-like).

Adam was intimately familiar with the story of Genesis. He was God's first human creation, was addressed by God (see for instance, Genesis 1:28 and 2:16), and served as the world's first taxonomist, having been commanded to name each and every animal.

Adam and his wife Eve were the pinnacles of creation. They shone with a luminescence and had transcendental vision. They were exalted in every way. They did not eat like animals, they did not communicate like animals and they did not copulate like animals. They received instructions about "the birds and the bees" from God Himself.

It was only when subsequent generations deviated from the exclusive worship of God, interesting themselves in the service of the celestial bodies and eventually diverging totally to idolatry and paganism, that God's lessons of "the birds and the bees" were forgotten. Human beings perverted sex. It was then that sex became trivialized, animalistic and all pervasive; it was then that all the theories of cosmogony, I mentioned earlier, took form. God, religion, and ordinary living became sensualized and sexualized.[104]

The giving of the Torah 1,518 years after Adam's death reinstated the true origins of the universe and de-sexualized God—"In the Beginning of God's creation of the Heaven and the Earth"—by His will, not through any sexual behavior. The Torah gave laws regulating sex. As Dennis Prager writes, the Torah placed controls on sexual activity. It could no longer dominate religion and social life. It was to be sanctified—which in Hebrew means "separated"—from the world and placed in the home, in the bed of husband and wife. The Torah's restricting of sexual behavior enabled society to progress. Along with ethical monotheism, the revolution begun by the Torah when it declared war on the sexual practices of the world wrought the most far-reaching changes in history. In the Egyptian *Syballine Oracles*, written probably

---

[104]   The preceding ideas were based on Dennis Prager's article *Why Judaism and later Christianity Rejected Homosexuality* (Crisis, 8:11, September 1993) and Dr. J.H. Hertz in *The Pentateuch* (Soncino Press, London)

between 163 and 45 B.C., the author compared Jews to the other nations: The Jews "are mindful of holy wedlock, and they do not engage in impious intercourse with male children, as do Phoenicians, Egyptians, and Romans, specious Greece and many nations of others, Persians and Galatians and all Asia."

Adam and Eve

The primordial human being, called "Adam," was a hermaphrodite. Both sexes were conjoined in one body, as the Torah states: "God created Adam in His image. In the image of God, He created him, male and female He created them." [Gen. 1:27]

This verse is the basis for the distinction between the sex lives of all other creatures, on the one hand, and human marriage, on the other hand. Other creatures are also divided into two sexes, but in their case both sexes came into being *simultaneously* and *independently* of one another. They need one another only for the purpose of breeding, not for any intrinsic purpose. They do not need one another to fulfill their life's purpose: only for the purpose of breeding and for the time devoted to this one act do they seek and find one another. The human male and female, in contrast to animals, were created as one unit. They can fulfill their intrinsic purpose in this world only by reuniting.

Before the human specie was divided into male and female, the hermaphrodite Adam was subordinate to one Divine will. When human males and females reunite, through marriage, they must again subordinate their energies and aspirations to the service of a higher will.[105]

"Though all living creatures were created in two sexes," wrote Hirsch, "this fact is stressed only in the case of man in order to state the verity that both sexes, male and female, were created to be equally close to God, and equally in His image."

The two components of the human being, Adam and Eve, were created physiologically and psychologically different. In general, the human male is larger and stronger than the female, with more aggressive hormones coursing through his bloodstream, because his role is to

---

[105]   Based on Samson Raphael Hirsch in *The Pentateuch (Judaica Press, New York, 1986) p.8*

protect and provide for his family. The human female has the components to birth and nurse babies, with more nurturing hormones in her bloodstream, because her role is to nurture. The Torah records that Eve is to be Adam's *"ezer k'negdo,"* which means his "helpmate opposite him." The classical commentator Rashi explains this term: "If he is worthy, she is a helpmate; if he is not worthy, she opposes him." In other words, the female is supposed to keep the male on track, supporting him when he is moving in the right direction, and opposing him when he is moving in the wrong direction. Thus she enables him to reach his full potential, and helps him discover the real him.

Physical vs. Spiritual

That God created the human being in His image means that the human was created to be God-like. No animal was created "in the image of God." Thus God endowed the original human with something from Himself. The defining element of the human being is this endowment from God.

According to Kabbalah a purely physical creature is endowed with life due to the presence of a *Nefesh Beheimis,* which functions according to instinct. The purely spiritual being is called *Neshama*, which functions according to a higher realm. That the human being was created "in the image of God" means that the human being was a *Neshama*.

The role of the physical body for the original human being, which functioned through the powers of *Nefesh Beheimis*, was as a mere suit to clothe the soul, the *Neshama*. A shield was necessary to protect the divine soul in a terrestrial world, just like a spacesuit is necessary to protect an astronaut in space. In another words, the physical body was not fused together with the soul. Like a man or woman who undresses after a day at work, Adam and Eve were able to undress themselves from their bodies. Adam and Eve wore their physical bodies like we wear garments; they express us, but they are not part of us.

In this elevated spiritual context, there was no shame surrounding sexuality. Sexuality was a process as natural as eating, drinking, and sleeping. Just as there was no need to cover other organs of the body, such as the nose and mouth, there was no need to clothe the reproductive organs. Thus, the Torah tells us, that Adam and Eve were naked.

This is not to say that Adam and Eve were free of all temptation. However, temptation in the Garden of Eden was externalized in the person of the snake. While Adam and Eve had no inner conflicts, because good and evil were transparent to them, the snake's mission was to challenge them to disobey God.

The evil inclination wanted to cause a tension between the spiritual and the physical. Its goal was to insure that Adam and Eve no longer experience physicality as a means to spirituality, but rather as an end unto itself. Sex for Adam and Eve would no longer be an innocent, physical act that led to the greatest spiritual delights, but rather an act of exclusive physicality, tinged with lust and baseness. Eating for Adam and Eve would no longer be an innocent, physical act performed to infuse them with energy to serve their Creator, but as an end unto itself—eating for the sake of eating. This evil inclination desired to strip Adam and Eve of their uniquely human, Divine innocence and inject animalistic tendencies into their personas, where an act in the physical domain would be a strictly physical act with no human, higher component.

God gave Adam and Eve one, and only one, commandment: not to eat from the fruit of the Tree of Knowledge of Good and Evil. The Tree of Knowledge of Good and Evil represented the admixture of the Nefesh Beheimis (purely physical) and the Neshama (spiritual). Devouring from the fruit of the Tree of Knowledge would inject the struggle of good and evil directly into the human being.

When Adam and Eve defied God and ate from the forbidden tree, their physical bodies synthesized with and overshadowed their souls. This synthesizer is called *Ruach*. This fusion spurred tremendous turmoil and conflict within the human being.

Eating from the forbidden tree wrought a powerful metamorphosis in Adam and Eve. Their luminescent souls were now eclipsed by and amalgamated with bodies of gross physicality, rendering the light of the soul virtually invisible. Immediately upon sinning, Adam and Eve sensed this loss of innocence and holiness. For the first time, Adam and Eve had awareness that they were naked. The Torah states: "They knew they were naked." Clothing became necessary in order to cover the body so that human beings didn't become thoroughly distracted by the body to the detriment of the soul. In other words, in order to equalize the manifold choices between body and soul, since the soul was now covered (by the body), it was only fair that the body should also be covered (by clothes).

Modesty is so important because as it hides parts of the body, it defines the physical body as subservient to the soul. In this manner, a person is not labeled, judged, or "loved" (see introduction) solely according to their physical form or characteristics. The less modesty in a society, the further that society moves from Eden.

Eden was nirvana, a veritable paradise. There is a way to restore ourselves to Eden. This can be accomplished through a counter metamorphosis, meaning that the soul must gradually be reinstated to its original exalted state as the primary component of the human being. This means that every physical act must be viewed not as an end in itself, but as the means to a loftier, spiritual goal.

We must perform *transcendental physicality*. For example, we must engage in our occupation not merely to earn money for the sake of earning money, but rather as a means to reveal our souls. We accomplish this by earning that money respectfully and ethically, and using that money in wholesome ways that will contribute to the true enhancement of our families and our communities. The more we do this, the more the soul becomes visible.

The same is possible for all physical acts. One can eat hedonistically, for the sake of eating, or one can eat in order to be healthy and energetic to serve God and humanity. Sex too can be a selfish and exploitative act, or can be a transcendental act, the most elevated way to totally unite with one's beloved spouse.

In this segment of the book I will introduce you to a new way of life: to a more profound, enriching, and happier sexuality, to a higher existence and a more pleasurable state of being.

Fifteen

Heavenly Sex
& Pleasure

"Sometimes now I sit back and say, 'What was I thinking before I was thinking?'"

—Madonna in Ladies Home Journal (June, 2005)

How do we know what kind of sacrifices and work are necessary in order to get the most out of life? The truth is we don't know. If we want to know how to get the most out of a car, we consult its owner's manual. If we were to purchase a computer, we would consult its system manual. We trust the author of the manual because he/she is the creator and designer of the system. So, for example, because Bill Gates is the originator and architect of the Microsoft Windows operating system, he surely knows what works well with the system or what can corrupt or be detrimental to the system. Mr. Gates even wrote an entire manual explaining the operating system for Microsoft Windows.

Our Creator is the "Bill Gates" of our bodies. As the designer, creator and architect of our bodies, God knows exactly what will achieve us ultimate reward and happiness. God also wrote an entire manual explaining the operating system of the human being. This "instruction & operating manual for human beings" is the Torah. So if God tells us that a certain pleasure or activity may cause a spiritual virus, we can be sure that it must be toxic to our souls. God's instruction manual for human beings—the Torah—contains all the details on permitted and forbidden pleasures.

My brother told me about a pilot from a commercial airliner who walked into a bar. The pilot, dressed in an impeccably pressed uniform, looked like he would be flying imminently. He slapped a twenty-dollar bill on the bar and demanded two swigs of whiskey. The bartender, after looking the pilot up and down, refused to give him the drink. The pilot, irate, cursed the bartender and left in a huff.

Twenty minutes later, a pregnant woman entered the bar. She requested a drink of Drambuie. The bartender explained to the woman that he could not, in fair conscience, sell her the drink. The woman took offense, and retorted that it is a free country and she had every right to do what she wanted. The bartender would not budge. Out walked the angry, pregnant woman.

A short while later, a soldier entered the bar and ordered a couple beers. The bartender politely, but adamantly, refused to give the soldier the drinks. The soldier shouted at the bartender that he had no right to deprive him of the little pleasure he wished to have. The bartender told the soldier that because the nation was on high alert for terrorism, it would be unethical for the soldier to be operating without total clarity. The soldier left the bar perturbed and disappointed.

The next day, the pilot returned. He said to the bartender, "I am here to express my gratitude. As you have surely heard, a jetliner crashed last night killing hundreds of passengers. A preliminary investigation indicates that the pilot was drunk. As you know, that pilot could have been me. Thank you for saving me."

Shortly afterwards, the pregnant woman entered the bar. She said, "After I left your bar yesterday, I encountered a woman wheeling a retarded child in a stroller. The mother of the baby sized me up and told me, 'I want you to know that in my last trimester of pregnancy, I downed too much alcohol and this child is the result.' I am here to thank you for stopping me from causing such potential damage to my baby."

Later on, the soldier reappeared at the bar. The bartender eyed the soldier as he made his way to a stool at the bar. After sitting down, the soldier told the bartender that one of his fellow soldiers had drunk one too many and had accidentally shot his own compatriots, seriously injuring three of them. He had come to express sincere gratitude to the bartender for safeguarding him from something he could have forever regretted.

I thought my brother created a great story but his message is even better. Put yourself, he says, in the shoes of the pilot, pregnant lady, or soldier in the story. Next, replace the bartender with the ultimate bartender, God. Finally, substitute the alcoholic beverages with any conceivable pleasure you have ever wanted. Throughout life we demand pleasures, many of them self-destructive or destructive of others. God is like the bartender who refuses us those pleasures. We get mad at God or we deny God. Sometimes it takes years, sometimes even a lifetime, for us to realize that God knows best.

Salubrious Sex

God allows pleasures that are salubrious for our systems. Being human means that we aren't just sophisticated animals. Human beings are characterized by dignity and loftiness. In another words, because we are human, our actions must be guided by a higher ideal.

Our humanity is found in our minds. Neurologically and physiologically, the mind is also the center where we experience pleasure. Kabbalah teaches that the seat of our souls is also in our minds. Because our soul is in our mind, holiness and wisdom are attainable through the mind.

The pleasures that emanate from—and come to—our minds have to be those that further our being human; otherwise they can prove hazardous to our operating system. As lofty as we may be, we are also sexual beings. Therefore it is incumbent on us to learn which kind of sex furthers our being human and which kind of sex doesn't.

Proper sex benefits our souls. It furthers our humanity.

Proper sex is viewed by God as not only holy, but as an essential exercise in being and becoming human. Contrary to making us more animalistic, proper sex makes us more angelic. While it is unnatural and unhealthy for a human being to indulge in physical pleasures based only on instinct, like an animal, *human sex* is done with foresight and care. It can't be performed according to whim, or arbitrarily. It can't be performed if not sanctioned by our Designer. It is done with preparation and the right concentration of spiritual power and energy.

The very first instance of sex recorded in the Bible was between Adam and Eve. The verb employed to depict this first cohabitation is, "And Adam *knew* Eve." The "Instruction Manual for Human Beings" formula for sex is, surprisingly, knowledge. The very facet that differentiates man from animal—mind power and deep knowledge— is the recipe for human sex. Thus, sex between humans is supposed to be on a totally different level than that practiced by animals. Human sex is about *knowledge.*

This knowledge requires one to ponder the repercussions of every potential sexual encounter. It requires the human being to make deliberate, rational, methodical choices and exert control when necessary. When Bill Clinton was asked what he was thinking when he began his adulterous relationship with Monica Lewinsky, he said, "most personal encounters are not entirely rational." Clinton was admitting that he functioned according to whim and instinct instead of knowledge.

In order for sex to be truly human, it must be Divinely sanctioned. There must be a covenant between a man and a woman, a pact of marriage that consecrates their sexual union. Kabbalah teaches that before the souls of a future couple come into earthly existence, they are one soul. Immediately prior to descending into this world, the soul is divided. Through marriage, it is reunited. Sex without marriage misses the mark because, absent the consecration, the souls are not reunited. Sex between a *married couple* is a momentous, holy, and joyous occasion, because it creates union on all levels: the physical, emotional, intellectual, and spiritual levels.

Ultimate togetherness, ultimate closeness, ultimate unity, ensues only when God is placed in front of a relationship. If you want to have true harmony, love, and fulfillment with your soul mate, you have to have a consecrated relationship.

God gave man an inherent feeling to be modest. It is natural to protect and camouflage the reproductive organs. Thus these organs are almost universally referred to as "private parts." They are to remain private and sacred—reserved for the consecrated moment with the consecrated partner.

Celibacy?

While other religions view sex as vile and base, and therefore promulgate celibacy as an ideal, the "Instruction Manual for Human Beings" states that marriage is the ideal. The Torah states that a life without marrying is less holy and less complete. In Torah law only a married man was allowed to be a high priest, and only a man who had children could sit as a judge on the Jewish Supreme Court, the Sanhedrin.

In the holiest site in the great Temple of Jerusalem stood the Holy Ark. Inside the Holy Ark the original tablets of the Ten Commandments were placed. Carved on top of the Holy Ark was the golden image of a male and female cherub in passionate embrace. It was from this spot that in times of peace, God's glory would shine forth. This signified the holiness of the sexual communion of male and female.

The home in Talmudic literature is called a "miniature Temple." The Temple had areas of ascending holiness: the courtyard, the sanctuary (which included the outer chamber or "the holy"), and finally the inner chamber, "the holy of holies." The portals of the home are like the courtyard of the Temple. The inside of the home is the sanctuary. The bedroom is the "holy of holies." What goes on in the bedroom is *the highest level of holiness possible*. This can't be stressed too much: The sexual union of a married couple is holy—in fact, holy of holies.

Consecrated sexuality can lift a couple to the highest realms of spirituality. The holier or more spiritual the couple is, the greater purity and holiness they will inject into becoming "one flesh." In this special moment of conjugation, the *Shechina,* the Divine glory itself, is present.

We see that the Torah attitude towards healthy sex is that it not only can be extremely pleasurable, but it is actually very holy. This attitude contrasts to other religions, such as Catholicism, Hinduism, and Buddhism, which regard sex as a necessary evil. The Catholic priest, the Hindu *sannyasin,* and the Buddhist monk are the holiest practitioners of their respective religions. All of them are celibate. Such celibacy is in violation of the first commandment in the Bible: "Be fruitful and multiply."

It was not until the eleventh century that celibacy was instituted by the Catholic Church. According to Diarmaid MaCulloch, author of *The Reformation: A History*,[106] there were two reasons for this enactment and both reasons were ignoble and reprehensible. Like today, in medieval times, the Church owned a lot of land. The fear was that the priests would bequeath the land to their children, causing the Church's coffers to suffer. The second motive was to elevate the status of the priest into a nonsexual being, meaning that the priest was God-like and free from temptation or lust.

America recently was reeling from the disclosure that many Catholic priests have been sexually abusing thousands of children. The harm inflicted by these immoral, sexually starved religious leaders is irreparable.

Here are the observations of a former "renunciate" member of a Hindu ashram:[107]

> The hardest part of life at the ashram was the lack of what our guru disdainfully called, "one-on-one relationships." The ideal of Eastern spiritual paths is celibacy. They assert that sexual relationships dissipate spiritual energy and that emotional attachments divert one's exclusive focus on God. For our ashram, composed mostly of men and women in their twenties, celibacy was a difficult, unrelenting challenge.

> Then, in 1984, during my fifteenth year at the ashram, I was disillusioned and unsettled by a series of scandals involving the most prestigious gurus. First the New Age world was shaken by the revelation that the Zen Roshi heading the San Francisco Zen Center had been having an affair with one of his married students.

> Next came a host of sexual allegations against the revered Swami

---

[106] Viking Press, June 2004

[107] Sara Levinsky Rigler, author of the manuscript, *A Bridge of Dreams*, a 640-page biography of Swami Paramananda.

Muktananda. After that, one guru after another fell like a game of dominos.

The July, 1985, issue of the "Yoga Journal" featured as its cover story: "Why Teachers Go Astray; Gurus, Sex, and Spirituality." It included an article by Buddhist teacher Jack Kornfield, who reported:

> According to this survey—which includes information on 54 teachers—sexual relations form a part of the lives of 39 of them . . . Significantly, 34 of the 39 teachers who are not celibate have had at least occasional sexual relationships with one or more students.

Back to the former ashram member:

> I was devastated. Here I was straining every nerve and muscle to follow the ideal of celibacy, while the most highly regarded proponents of the path couldn't hack it themselves! And what about the issue of truth? Almost all of those 39 teachers publicly espoused the importance of celibacy and pretended to be celibate.

Contrast all the above with the fact that God commanded Jewish males to circumcise, of all things, their sexual organ. Why?

> A stamp of holiness on what the world views as the most base of organs is there to illustrate that the ideal of saintliness is not realized by the ascetic who has "purged" himself from all sexual desires but, on the contrary, by him in whom those desires burn fiercest and yet, without being altogether starved, are tamed and governed.[108]

So the stamp of circumcision is there to remind us that sex comes with tremendous responsibility. A misuse of sex abuses the sanctity of the human being.

---

[108] Based on *Judaism and Christianity* by Trude Weiss-Rosemarin (Jewish Book Club, 1947)

As the great spiritual teacher Aryeh Kaplan wrote:[109]

> Through the covenant of circumcision, God gave Abraham and his descendents power over the transcendental plane. The most obvious case in which this occurs is in conception, where a soul is brought down into the world. Since the mark of the covenant is on the sexual organ, it gives the individual access to the highest spiritual realms, from which he can draw down the loftiest souls . . .

> The covenant of circumcision also represents the channeling of sexual energy. The sexual drive is one of the most powerful psychological forces in man, and when it is channeled along spiritual lines, it can help bring one to the highest mystical states. In giving the commandment of circumcision, God indicated that the emotions and desires associated with sex could be used for the mystical quest of the Divine on a transcendental plane.

Human sexuality, as well as any human craving, has to be expressed in a uniquely human fashion. As has been emphasized numerous times, the most marked human characteristic that distinguishes us from animals is our charge to be spiritual. If we are sexual in a distinctly human way, then we are not only furthering our own individual humanity, but also we are making transcendental spiritual strides, which cause dramatic positive effects for all of humanity.

Self-Control

> I hurt people by confusing them. One minute I was saying believe in yourself and the next I was saying, 'Just be sexually provocative for the sake of it.' Now that's confusing. Ultimately, none of us wants to be judged because of the way we look. We want people to appreciate us for who we are on the inside. So I didn't exactly help people by being an exhibitionist."

—Madonna in Ladies Home Journal (June, 2005)

---

[109]   In his commentary to *The Book of Creation* (Weiser, Maine, 1991) p.37

I will never forget the story about a man who wanted to buy his septuagenarian mother a unique birthday present. He went to a pet shop and bought a parrot that spoke six languages. He paid $10,000 for this amazing bird, and another $100 to have it delivered to her on her birthday. That afternoon, he called her and asked her how she liked the bird. "It's delicious," she answered. "I'm just finishing it now."

This is precisely what the sexual revolution has done to human beings. Humans have amazing gifts of spirit and intellect, but the sexual revolution has relegated all humans to mere bodies—sexual objects fated "for consumption."

Pundits have wrongly blamed America's immoral woes on foreigners and immigrants. Just recently, on February 13, 2003 a full-fledged American woman dentist was convicted of murdering her husband, a very American orthodontist. She ran him over, two times, with her Mercedes-Benz. Why? He was having an affair with his secretary. This is definitely troubling but it gets worse. During the trial, the entire affair was analyzed in vivid detail. It was publicized why the dead orthodontist thought that his secretary was a better love partner than his wife was. It got so perverted and vile, that his wife and secretary's respective anatomies' were verbally dissected to illustrate his sexual preferences. This, of course, was broadcasted on the national news media—prime time.

Since the advent of the sexual revolution, Western culture has come to regard both men and women as sex objects. Advertisements and entertainment pander to the grossest sexual blandishments. Even the "fine art" produced today can rarely be found without portrayals of the female or male physique. For example, a large painting adorning the wall of the dining room in a "family hotel" showed a vase of brightly colored flowers; a second look revealed, amidst the free-form design on the vase itself, a prancing nude woman. No aspect of life in Western culture has remained untouched—and uncorrupted—by the pervasive sexual predominance.

Viewing human beings as objects or measuring beauty according to external form is the greatest affront to our humanity. The beauty of the human being is really in the inherent value of the human being.

Imagine, for example, that Susan is preparing for a job interview. Her friend Nancy is there to assist her in choosing an outfit. Nancy recommends that Susan wear a tank top and mini-skirt for the interview. Susan looks incredulously at her friend, and sputters, "Are you for real? I don't want to get the job based on the shape of my body. I want to be judged on the merits of who I really am."

Nancy responds, "So why do you wear this type of clothing when dating men?"

Many women epitomize this self-contradictory stance when they dress in a way that draws attention to their bodies and then insist that they want to be regarded as more than a sex object. Have you ever noticed that female lawyers invariably appear in court wearing dignified and modest suits or dresses? Obviously, when a woman wants to be respected for her intellect, she instinctively covers her body.

According to Kabbalah, the secret of human potential is alluded to in the name that God chose for humans. God called the first human being "Adam." The etymology of this word is from the Hebrew word "adama," which means "earth." This is odd because one would think that our earthly origin should be secondary, rather than our identifying characteristic.

Think about the earth. Consider the vast potential for growth and nourishment that lays dormant in the earth. Unless the earth is tilled and cultivated, however, the great potential cannot be actualized. The human being, too, is full of potential, but it takes work to actualize it.

When we consider how to keep ourselves sexually moral in the face of ever-present hormones, we should reflect on this point. The struggle to preserve our humanness and that of others requires real labor and toil. We must overcome our own passions and rule the body with the intellect. This requires discipline and hard work, but the result is a fruitful life, like a well-tended orchard.

In contrast to the majority of the animal kingdom, the human being is not born fully functional. It takes years for the human being to become competent to fend for himself. According to a renowned educator:

> The explanation of his singularity is that it is precisely because man is paramount, strictly because he is born in the Almighty's image, he is born incomplete. Man was granted the divine and unique opportunity to become a meaningful partner in his own creation. He gives birth to himself in a way, as he forms his own self by expanding and developing all of his life, shaping his own destiny. Every person, every event, every step we take, no matter how feeble it may seem, is of cosmic importance . . . Since I have the mission to create myself, and to produce my life, I cannot be happy in a role that is not mine. Man was meant to produce, not merely be produced.[110]

This is in total contrast to the animal. The animal is called in Hebrew "bahema," which is a contraction of two words "bah" and "ma," which mean, "Whatever is in it, it is." This suggests that the animal is genetically preprogrammed to act in the way that it is supposed to. The animal stands exposed and naked, conveying no sense of privacy or mystery, to demonstrate the idea that, "What you see is what you get."

The magic in the human being—the real you—is thus deeply correlated with your modesty. God created the human being to take his profound worth and build upon it, elevating himself to the finest expression of creation. When the human being sheds his clothes, exposing his sexuality, he trivializes his worth.

A person who wants to use his or her intellect to achieve his or her full potential would do well to minimize temptation. In contemporary Western culture, this will require keeping a distance from those ubiquitous vehicles that are designed to arouse the sexual impulse: provocative Internet sites and media venues.

Torah law, quite cognizant of our physical makeup and drives, gave certain rules to protect us from self-destructing and destroying others. There are three main guidelines that the Talmud, based on the Torah, promulgates:

1)   It is imperative for a man not to be secluded with a woman who is

---

[110]   A. Kaufman, Consequential Conversations. . . Without Being Confrontational, *Timeless Parenting* (Mesorah Publications, New York, 2000)

not his wife, daughter, mother, grandmother or sister. Likewise, it is imperative for a woman not to be secluded with a man who is not her husband, son, father, grandfather, or brother.

This is a sure-fire way to keep compromising situations from developing. Had Bill Clinton observed this rule, he would not have provided cause for his impeachment.

This prohibition is waived when the situation affords an opportunity for other adults to enter at any time, such as in an elevator or a busy office, or even at home during daylight hours when the door is unlocked (unless you live in a remote place where no one is likely to intrude).

2) **"Don't speak with a woman unnecessarily."[111] Do not engage in excessive talk with a woman who isn't your wife.**

Chatting builds conviviality, which can lead to attraction. How many married men and women have considered themselves immune to philandering, only to later fall into a romantic attachment with someone who was initially a casual friend?

3) **Limit touching a member of the opposite sex who is not your spouse, child, or parent. We are warm-blooded human beings, and physical touch can lead to sexual temptation.**

As Sandra Ann Taylor writes,[112] "When you touch, your bodies produce oxytocin, which creates a feeling of serenity. . . . Physically and chemically, it bonds you and makes you feel closer."

Lest anyone think that these rules are useful only for the super-sexed, stop and consider the last romantic movie you saw. Most likely, the attraction started in one of these three ways: Through being alone together, striking up a conversation, or simply touching. A common

---

[111]   Talmud, Avos 1:5, also known as Ethics of the Fathers (*Pirkei Avoth*)

[112]   *Secrets of Attraction: The Universal Laws of Love, Sex and Romance*, quoted in Readers Digest, November 2002

best-selling novel, *The Winner*, by David Baldacci illustrates this progression:

> She winced slightly as he said her name . . . She finally reached up and lightly caressed his fingers with her own . . . . She looked up at him, and their eyes did not budge form each other as their fingers exchanged touches that were suddenly electrifying both their bodies . . .

I take the liberty to omit what happened next, but I believe I have provided enough clues.

4) A final device to win the battle with your hormones: Always remember that "Somebody" is watching.

Rabbi Israel Meir Kagan (1828-1933) once hired a driver to take him to a distant town. As they were passing an orchard, the driver noticed ripe fruit hanging from the trees. The driver stopped the carriage and requested that Rabbi Kagan warn him if anybody approached. Just as the driver was about to pick some fruit, Rabbi Kagan shouted, "Somebody's watching, somebody's watching!" The driver ran right back to his carriage. As he started driving away, he looked around to see who was watching, and saw no one. "Why did you shout that someone was watching?" he angrily asked.

Rabbi Kagan responded: "God was watching."

Marriage

Today marriage in the Western world is an embattled institution. Statistics suggest that one in two marriages will end in divorce. This leads to families in crisis. Children growing up in single-parent homes are prone to a battery of emotional and psychological hazards. This is terribly dangerous for society.

The currently dominant school of American criminology holds that early-childhood experience is the greatest diagnostic for determining the level of subsequent criminality. According to this theory, most people do not make day-to-day choices about whether or not to commit crimes based on the balance of rewards and risks, as the rational-choice school sometimes suggests. The vast majority of people obey the law, particularly with regard to serious offenses, out of habit that was learned relatively early in life.[113]

According to Benjamin B. Wolman, a leading psychologist who has studied sociopathy for over 50 years, sociopathic behavior usually stems from inadequate parenting and abusive childhood environments. In his book *Antisocial Behavior*, he emphasizes: "*The vast majority of sociopaths are not born sociopaths.* Children who are exposed to parental neglect and/or abuse and children who witness interparental violence turn sociopathic. Inadequate guidance, lack of moral encouragement, and frequent exposure to pathological selfishness foster sociopathic personality development."

The situation of family life in America is so dire that President George W. Bush has allocated a billion and a half dollars to marriage education and retention programs.

The reason why marriage is in disarray is because the age-old institution of marriage has been exploited and sabotaged. Marriage has become just as disposable as disposable cameras. Western culture has portrayed marriage as a big exercise of vanity and self-gratification. Marriage is not about disposability; marriage is not about transient romance and love.

Family and marriage are the bedrock of healthy living. There is absolutely nothing more important for the viability and preservation of society then family and marriage. The very first instruction that the Torah gives man is to get married and build a family. This imperative makes man into a giver. He cannot be a selfish, solitary, member of society but must engage in selfless, responsible acts of loving, supporting and nurturing a marriage and family.

Most of the time, when we say we love something we really mean we love *ourselves*. We love the gratification and pleasure that we get out of those things. When we say we love a food item, such as pizza, we are really saying that we love the fact that the pizza makes *us* happy. If we loved the pizza we wouldn't allow our gastric juices to devour and destroy it. When we say we love a person, we are really saying we love what the person does for *us* and how they meet our conscious and

---

[113]   Francis Fukuyama in *The Great Disruption: Human Nature and the Reconstitution of Social Order* (Free Press, 1999)

unconscious needs. That is not love. The Western ideal of love and romance really translates into selfishness and egoism.

In Hebrew, the etymology of the word for "love" is "Hav"—to "give." True love is about giving, nurturing, and understanding. The ultimate ideal in marriage is where both partners espouse roles as true lovers—givers. When each spouse says, "What can I give, what can I invest into this relationship" and not "What can I get out of this relationship," ultimately both spouses will be recipients of each other's love. So while both husband and wife end up receiving, their mindset is strictly giving. The outcome is that they are truly loving one another.

As Professor Lawrence Keleman wrote:

> By staying married Jewish couples choose to accept all the challenges of dealing with their spouse, long after the masks of romance and the challenge of the chase have fallen away— when staying married means finding pleasure among ever-increasing responsibilities rather then seeking pleasure as an end in itself.

The components of the Torah ideal of marriage were enumerated by Maimonides[114] more than 800 years ago:

> The Talmud teaches that a man must honor his wife <u>more</u> than he honors himself. He must love and cherish her as much as he does himself. He should spoil her, according to his financial means. He should never frighten her and his communication with her should be pleasant. He shouldn't act depressed or tense in her presence.

> A woman must exceedingly honor her husband, almost to the point of reverence. . . . He should be in her eyes like a minister or king. She should please him and cast away anything that upsets him.

Research has proven that the Divine model, the Torah ideal of marriage and family works quite well.

---

[114] Maimonides, *Laws of Marriage*, 15:19-20

Sixteen

Deindividuation

Awoman called in to a radio show recently admitting to having been convicted of a felony. Her crime? While in college she abused methamphetanine (crystal) with needles. She sounded like an intelligent young lady, which prompted the host of the show to ask her why she, a seemingly bright, ambitious person, succumbed to taking drugs. Her answer was axiomatic, "Because everybody else in college was doing it."

People in crowds can exhibit immoral, destructive behavior that they would never indulge in when they are alone. When in large, anonymous crowds, they often lose all awareness of their individuality and subjugate themselves to the mood and actions of the crowd. Psychologists have dubbed this behavior, "deindividuation."[115]

An example of this took place when the Chicago Bulls won the NBA Championship a decade ago. Caught up in the collective exhilaration of the crowd, thousands of fans turned the victory celebration into bedlam and chaos. They rioted, set fires, overturned cars, and caused inestimable damage.

---

[115] Festinger et al. . . (1952)

Cults encourage the deindividuation of their members in order to promote conformity and allegiance to the group. Sometimes they require uniforms to eliminate the member's distinctive identity. The assumption is that the more a person is deindividuated, the more he or she will accept the ideology of the cult.

One of the first tactics employed in debriefing captured enemy combatants is the deindividuation of the subjects. The psychology behind this is that when the person is stripped of his individuality he becomes vulnerable, defenseless, and confused.

Deindividuation is the antithesis of the Torah's concept of human beings. The Talmud explains that each human being was created in total uniqueness. Although earthly kings mint coins and they are all identical to each other, God, the King of kings, fashioned every man to be distinctive and unique. The Talmud is saying that individuality is the hallmark of being human.

Unfortunately, today many of us are self-induced victims of deindividuation. We have a propensity to disengage our minds, and let others such as Madison Avenue, the fashion industry, television, movies, and the Internet do our thinking for us. We allow ourselves to fall prey to cultural trends and fads that are alien to our core selves. A person must exert great effort and self-mastery to buck the trends, and not allow others to define his/her dress, actions, and attitudes.

Often one's own peer group can be more perilous than the Hollywood trendsetters. Because we feel comfortable in our familiar group, our individuality does not feel threatened. This is when we are most vulnerable to negative influence.

When Jackie Robinson became the first African-American baseball player, he faced tremendous hostility from his own white teammates, the Brooklyn Dodgers. Robinson was scorned, hit, and mocked. He even received death threats. Only one member of the team, PeeWee Reiss, refused to join in the collective harassment. When others poked fun, Reiss defended Robinson. This elicited the group's ire against Reiss himself. He was branded a "nigger lover" and a coward. In fact, Reiss was the strongest man on the team, because he held fast to his principles regardless of what everyone else was doing.

Many of us can learn from Reiss. Many of us know deep down in our hearts that what others are doing is wrong, yet we conform and adopt negative and destructive ways of acting, speaking, and dressing, due to peer pressure. The desire to be "cool" has anaesthetized the minds of millions of American youth, cajoling them into smoking cigarettes, taking drugs, and hooking up, whether or not they derive any real joy from these self-destructive activities.

A somber parable points out the potential damage of peer pressure: There were four monkeys on a tree. The first three died and fell off the tree into a ravine. The fourth monkey jumped off the tree into the ravine, killing himself. He just had to be like the other monkeys.

Dr. Ariel Knafo of Ben-Gurion University's education department asserts that drug use is largely the result of conformity. A study he conducted found that most of those who choose to start taking drugs do so under peer pressure. According to Dr. Knafo, "Friends and environment very much control a person's decisions. Give me the name of the school in which a student learns and I can tell you pretty accurately if that student uses drugs or not."

To buck the trend, a student must have a strong internal moral compass. As Dr. Knafo says, "In environments where drug use is common, the values of the students become a primary factor in determining whether he or she will be affected by their environment." In other words, personal morality is the only counterbalance to peer pressure.

Some time ago, on October 10, 1994, *Newsweek* published a letter by a 14-year-old girl named Sabrina F. Hall. Although this letter addresses the issue of smoking, it is applicable to any other peer-pressure-induced addiction. She wrote:

> Since I've smoked, I can hardly run around the block without getting out of breath. My mom quit smoking 18 years ago and my dad stopped 14 years ago. My mom now has cancer, and my dad has had three heart attacks. My grandma quit nine years ago, and she has emphysema. Not only that—my two grandfathers died from the results of smoking. After all this you

would think I'd know better than to continue. Teenagers who think smoking is cool or who want to try it; don't! It might make you feel calmer when you are really worked up, but twenty years from now you could find yourself really calmed down. You, too, could get emphysema, lung cancer, mouth cancer and much more.

Not all pleasures are truly pleasurable. Not all friends are good friends. A prominent educator writes, "If people are enjoying themselves at present, but they are headed for disaster, what is the present enjoyment really worth? It is the pleasure of a man who enjoys the breeze coming through the open window of his car as he drives off a bridge."[116]

Standing Up

The Torah idealizes peace, but not at the price of integrity. If one is with a group of people who are indulging in a forbidden activity— anything from gossiping to sniffing cocaine, the Torah obligates one to stand up and either admonish the group or leave. The Torah expects one not only to protect himself from negative behaviors, but also to at least attempt to correct his friends, however unpopular this makes one.

The Torah exhorts us: "In a place where there are no men, be a man."[117] This demands having the courage to go against the current.

I will never forget when back in 1986; Len Bias was the Atlantic Coast Conference player of the year. The Boston Celtics chose him as the first selection of the National Basketball Association draft. He was offered a multi-million dollar contract. The night before signing this major deal, Len partied with friends in his college dormitory room. That night he collapsed and died. Traces of cocaine were found in his urine, and the resulting investigation led to charges against three friends who admitted using the drug with him.

What if just one of these so-called "friends" had stood up and protested the use of drugs that night? An entire lifetime of achievement and success could have been saved.

---

[116]   A. Kaufman, Consequential Conversations . . . Without Being Confrontational, *Timeless Parenting* (Mesorah Publications, New York, 2000)

[117]   Talmud, Avos 2:6

Whose Body Is It?

Try to tell a teenager that she shouldn't engage in self-destructive activities such as smoking, drugs, and hooking up, and she'll probably answer: "It's my body. I can do with it what I please."

The Torah disagrees. It commands: "Protect your physical vitality exceedingly well." Maimonides considered it a religious obligation to keep the body healthy and strong.

The Midrash tells a story about the great sage Hillel the Elder. His students saw him leave the hall of study and asked him where he was going. "I am going to do a holy act," he replied.

"Which holy act?" they questioned.

"To bathe in the bathhouse," was his answer.

"That's a holy act?"

"Yes," replied the sage. "The servant who cares for the king's articles on display washes and polishes them. Not only is he remunerated for his work; he is also regarded highly because he is in the service of the king. We are God's emissaries, created in His image. How much more so are we responsible to care for our bodies?"

Our bodies are on loan to us from our Creator. One day we will have to return them. It is similar to leasing a car. The leaser has the use of the car, but if he damages it, then, when the time comes to return the car, the leasing company will extract payment.

The Torah forbids people from placing their bodies in unnecessary danger. Three commandments are dedicated to this idea.[118] The Talmud says that whoever damages his body loses his portion in the next world.

Smoking, drugs, promiscuous sex, and obesity all pose grave dangers to the body.

Researchers at the Centers for Disease Control and Prevention in Atlanta found that sexual behavior results in three times as much premature death and disability in the U.S. as it does any other wealthy, industrialized country. Overall, sexual behavior accounted for 6 percent of all deaths and disabilities in the U.S. in 1998.

---

[118]   Refer to Deuteronomy, 4:9 and ibid. Verse 15. A third commandment is in Genesis, 9:5.

Obesity is also a chronic health problem. Scientists estimate that approximately one-third (190,090) of the 570,280 cancer deaths expected to occur in 2005 will be related to poor nutrition, physical inactivity, overweight, obesity and other lifestyle factors.

According to a news report by the Associated Press on August 23, 2004, overweight or obese men are 50 percent to twice as likely as lean men to get colon cancer. For women, the extra risk is 20 to 50 percent.

On March 31, 2005 the American Cancer Society reported that more than 60 percent of all cancer deaths could be prevented if Americans stopped smoking, exercised more, ate healthier food and got recommended cancer screenings.

Americans could realistically cut the death rate in half, the report says.

"The American Cancer Society estimates that in 2005, more than 168,140 cancer deaths will be caused by tobacco use alone," the organization said in a statement.

"The issue is how many could you actually pull off in reality and half doesn't seem like a big stretch," Dr. Michael Thun, head of epidemiology for the non-profit group, said in an interview.

"If one could eliminate tobacco use, you would eliminate about half of cancer deaths. If you could help people maintain a healthy body weight and get more physical activity, that would be another 10 percent," he added.[119]

Overcoming Addiction

In his best selling book *Ecstasy*, Jungian psychologist Robert Johnson makes it clear that addiction is nothing more than a severely degraded substitute for the true experience of joy. Addiction represents a yearning, an aspiration a higher level of experience. People are unfortunately misled to believe that substances and chemicals can lead to true fulfillment. What they fail to realize is

---

[119]   Reuters, March 31, 2005

that the inner depths of their souls are reaching out for ultimate spiritual fulfillment. In *Overcoming Addiction*, Dr. Chopra writes that spiritual satisfaction is a fundamental necessity of life, comparable to the need for food. He echoes what the Torah says quite emphatically: *Man does not live by bread alone but must sustain himself by the spirituality of God's Word.*[120] This means that the state of our spiritual life has tremendous bearing on our physical and mental health. We need spirituality or what Dr. Johnson calls *ecstasy* in the same basic way that we need food, water and air.

---

[120]   Deuteronomy, 8:3

Seventeen

Darwin's Ancestors

O ne of the long term repercussions of the sexual revolution was that young people began to accustom themselves to "rights" verses "obligation." In "From Responsibility to Satisfaction" (*Psychology Today*, May, 1992) the author referred to the outcome as such: "Adolescents and young adults saw themselves as deserving more and owing less to their families."

This ricocheted quite negatively not only upon families, as anticipated, but also upon American culture. Children raised with such a gestalt, in such a milieu, could hardly be expected to engage in serious pursuits of academic perseverance and achievement. The situation was so desperate that in 1980, an eccentric multimillionaire inventor, Robert K. Graham started the Repository for Germinal Choice, more commonly known as the Nobel Prize sperm bank. The goal was to offer, free of charge, the sperm of Nobel Prize winners and other high I.Q. strictly Caucasian men to equally intelligent married women with sterile husbands.

In 1989, President George H. Bush lamented: "Yet, still, as a nation, let's face it, we've got to do better. We're not producing enough scientists and mathematicians and engineers. American universities confer only about 77,000 engineering degrees a year at the undergraduate level. And that's about the same number that Japan produces with a total population of only half our size."

The problem has exacerbated. In the fall of 2004 the president of the University of Maryland found himself doing something that none of his predecessors would have dreamed of trying. While on a trip to Taiwan, C. Dan Mote Jr. spent part of his time recruiting Taiwanese students to go to the United States for graduate school.

On June 24, 2005, *The New York Times* reported that 41 percent of all math and physical science graduate students in the U.S. are foreigners. In engineering the figure is 50 percent.

The *Chronicle of Higher Education* (7/9/2004) reported:

> University presidents, government officials, and heads of industry have joined together in a chorus of concern over the state of science and engineering in the United States. The danger signs are obvious, they say. Fewer U.S. citizens are getting doctorates in those fields. There is increasing competition from other countries for the foreign graduate students who once flocked to the United States. And those changes come when many argue that the United States needs more technically trained people to power its economy. In a report in May, the National Science Board reached the gloomy conclusion that "these trends threaten the economic welfare and security of our country."

Also emblematic of the sexual revolution was a seismic shift of values. The adolescent of the post sexual revolution era venerated sexual icons and athletes instead of elders, religious figures, and national heroes.

It is axiomatic from previous chapters that worshipping sex icons is not exactly conducive, but what about athletes?

In *Scientific American* (April 2005), Steve Mirsky sums up the favorite American sport, football, as follows: "A lot of massive guys violently accelerating into one another with devastating force." *Sports*

Illustrated (January, 31, 2005) provided incisive testimony by pro-football players about what goes on inside a pile, where there is a battle for the ball: "I've had guys go for the privates, guys try to put their elbow in my neck, guys reaching into my helmet." "The go to spot are the eyes and the family jewels." "Guys reach inside the facemask to gouge your eyes. But the biggest thing is the grabbing of the testicles. It is crazy."

We thought that there were values to be learned from the athlete: perseverance, practice, and stamina. It seemed that the average-Joe baseball player, could convert himself into a super-star, home run hitter. Then we were exposed to the truth: Barry Bonds was no icon of the relentless, tireless average-Joe. It was all due to steroids. Many famous athletes fooled us. They abused steroids and drugs to advance in their careers. They too were products of the post sexual revolution era, accustomed to "rights" versus "obligation."

The Solution

A Torah scholar was once traveling on an airplane. Sitting beside him was an agnostic professor. Throughout the trip the rabbi's children and grandchildren, who were accompanying him, checked to see if he needed any assistance. This profoundly impressed the professor. He told the rabbi that he had never seen such respect given to an elderly father and grandfather. "As a matter of fact," explained the professor, "my own children disregard me and treat me without respect."

The Torah scholar replied, "You are a believer in Darwin, who claims that our ancestors were primates. Therefore, the further your children trace their lineage, the closer they come to apes and monkeys. You are closer to the primates than they are. Therefore they have ill regard for you. In my case, on the other hand, we believe that the further we go back, the closer we come to Adam, the first man. I, therefore represent a generation closer to the holiness of Adam. And my children therefore have the utmost respect for me."

Regarding Adam, the Torah says, "And Hashem God formed the man . . . and He blew into his nostrils the soul of life."

The Zohar comments: "One who blows, blows from within himself." In another words, Adam's soul was from God's own "breath." This means that Adam, the original person, was animated by nothing less than God Himself! The implication of being descended from Adam, rather than an ape, is profound.

In order for us to revamp society and reintroduce morality, children have to be taught that they are not "smarter" than previous generations. Although it is obvious that more recent generations are more technologically advanced, children can be taught to appreciate that technological knowledge is not at all the same as wisdom. Children must learn that the generations that preceded them are wiser and holier, closer to the original Adam. The previous generations are closer to that Divine "breath."

In the Holy Temple in Jerusalem there was a candelabrum, a *menorah*, of solid gold. The wicks of the *menorah* came from a very odd source. They came from the clothing that no longer fit or was too worn for the priests to wear. Couldn't the opulent Temple treasury have afforded wicks of new material?

Obtaining the wicks from this source demonstrated something that we unfortunately lack in contemporary America, namely, continuity from previous generations. The wicks imparted to the visitors of the Temple a critical life lesson: We do not discard what is taught by older generations, but we perpetuate these ideas for our own generation. Judaism, for instance, is built upon what in Hebrew is called *mesorah*, heritage—a chain transmitted from parent to child.

This approach contrasts radically with the contemporary secular outlook. In his 2003 commencement speech, James O. Freedman, the President Emeritus of Dartmouth College, said that the purpose of a college education is "to question your father's values." It is little wonder that such a repudiation of tradition and heritage breeds the sometimes rampant immorality prevalent on college campuses.

The fifth commandment exhorts us to honor our parents. Upon close study of the Ten Commandments, one can discern a pattern. The first tablet, containing the first five commandments, comprises laws that relate to man's relationship with God. The second tablet, containing numbers six through ten, comprises laws that relate to man's relationship with his fellow human being. So the question can be posited why the commandment of honoring parents is in the first group. The answer is that one can never honor and revere God if he disrespects his parents.

When we contemplate our source, we realize that our immediate origins are from our parents while ultimately we emanate from God. If we reject the values of our parents, we will ultimately reject God. This is exactly why "Honor thy father and mother" was placed in the grouping of man's relationship with God.

It is up to us to teach our children about God. We must be their principle motivators for proper morals and ethics.

In his commentary to the Bible, S.R. Hirsch elaborates on this theme:

> Our knowledge and acknowledgment of historic truths depend on our having a tradition. The maintenance of that tradition in turn requires parents who will faithfully transmit it to their children, and children who are willing to accept from the hands of their parents . . . Through the father and mother God gives the child more than merely his physical existence. Parents in fact represent the tie that binds the child to the past of his people and that enables the child to be a religious man or woman.[121]

Noblesse Oblige

One of the most troubling episodes in the Torah is the punishment of Moses. After risking his life to stand up to Pharaoh, leading the Israelites out of Egypt, ascending to supernal heights to bring down the Torah for humanity, and serving the argumentative Israelite nation in the desert for forty years, Moses makes a single mistake. The people are thirsty; they have no water. Moses prays to God, who tells him to speak to the rock, and the rock will give forth water. The people start to rebel, and Moses becomes flustered. Instead of speaking to the rock,

---

[121]   Adapted from *The Pentateuch* (Judaica Press, New York, 1986) p. 284

he strikes it with his rod (as he had been instructed to do years before in a previous miracle of water). His punishment for this "disobedience" is that he cannot enter the Promised Land, but is allowed only to view it from the other side of the Jordan River.

When asked why Moses' punishment is so severe for a seemingly minor infraction, the Torah states: "A righteous person is judged to a hair's breath."

This means that the higher one's stature, the higher one's level of accountability. Imagine that a close friend and advisor to the king is accused of espionage. His fate will be much worse than that of a peasant accused of the same crime.

The same is true for us. If humans are descendents of monkeys, then we can expect very little of ourselves in the sphere of morality. If, however, humans were created "in the image of God," then both God and we rightfully have high expectations of our inner ability to choose to act morally.

The litmus test of true strength is measured by how powerful one is against one's instinct. How well one can control temptation, lust, attraction, anger or a compelling drive to do something unethical, is the barometer to how strong one is. As *The Ethics of the Fathers* declares: "Who is strong? The one who can overcome himself." The strength to make difficult choices, to resist temptation, and to act morally is a function of one's self-image. See yourself as inherently godly, and you will be amazed at the heights you can attain.

Money

Staying ethical in business requires tremendous strength. It will take a long time for innocent Americans to recover billions of dollars of losses because of reprehensible management at companies such as Lucent, Enron and WorldCom. In all three cases, distinguished corporate executives succumbed to the temptation for more wealth to be added to their already considerable fortunes. They were heedless of the loss of the thousands of people from whom they were actually stealing. These cases constitute a massive moral failure. They highlight the questions: How does one stay clean in business? How does one avoid becoming obsessed with the dollar?

A story told about Rabbi Elijah of Vilna, suggests an answer. R. Elijah taught that the purpose of life is moral growth. His opus was a book on ethics called *The Fair Scale*. Once R. Elijah was hosting a prestigious guest. He bedecked his dining-room table lavishly with delicate crystal and fancy china. Nobody noticed that the tablecloth extended onto the floor. The guest accidentally stepped onto the tablecloth, bringing everything down onto the floor with a clatter. The guest was appalled. R. Elijah immediately pacified his guest by stating that nothing had broken. In utter disbelief, the guest looked at the floor and saw that it was true. To his amazement, not a single vessel was so much as cracked or chipped. He demanded an explanation from the rabbi for this supernatural occurrence. The rabbi explained that, as holiness is impervious to harm, so when holiness is transferred to one's physical possessions it also protects them.

How can money become holy? Money that is earned through proper ethics and pure intention actually becomes sanctified. Thus, the Torah's goal of sanctifying the physical attains a lofty expression in the sanctification of physical possessions through the moral integrity of the process that earned them.

Of course, the force that undermines morality is selfishness. When one is more devoted to one's own self-gratification than to a moral standard, the result will be fiscal and moral catastrophes such as the Enron scandal.

Once a middle-class, kind, generous man named Jack inherited a large fortune. He quickly became reclusive and stingy. Charities he had contributed to when he was making a moderate salary now walked away from his mansion empty-handed. Jack's rabbi noticed the stark change in his character and invited him for a meeting. The rabbi showed Jack to the window and asked him what he saw. Jack replied that he saw many people on the street. Then the rabbi showed Jack a mirror and asked him what he saw. Jack replied that he saw only himself.

"What's the difference between these two pieces of glass, the window and the mirror?" the rabbi asked Jack. Jacked shrugged. "The only difference between them is a layer of silver. The window, absent any silver coating, allows you to see other people. But as soon as we add a coating of silver, all you can see is yourself."

Wealth can corrupt. Torah sources speak of "the test of wealth" as being much harder than "the test of poverty."

If one doesn't learn to sanctify wealth through acquiring it and distributing it according to the highest moral standards, then wealth can become an addiction, which destroys the moral fiber of its owner.

There is a simple method that you can utilize to ascertain whether you are controlling your money or whether your money is controlling you. Ask yourself these two questions: Do I have an insatiable appetite for more money or do I feel content with what I have? When giving charity, do I feel fulfilled or do I feel a sense of loss?

The Talmud[122] tells us, "Who is rich? He who is happy with what he has."

---

[122]   Talmud, Avos 4:1

Eighteen

Vodka Watered Down

The Midrash relates that a king who was a contemporary of Moses heard reports of how the Hebrew leader had faced off with Pharaoh, had won the freedom of his entire people, had worked miracles, and had revealed a lofty legal code. The king was intrigued, and decided to utilize physiognomy (a system that enables one to decipher character traits from facial features) to ascertain whether Moses' reputation was fact or lore.

The king sent artists to the Sinai Desert to paint Moses' portrait. After the artists returned from their long journey with the portrait in hand, the experts in physiognomy went to work analyzing Moses' character. Their results were shocking. According to their proficient analysis, the character in the portrait was a robber, a murderer, and a deceitful person.

The king was enraged. Obviously, he inferred, the artists had painted the face of some vagabond they had encountered rather than making the long journey into the desert to find the great Moses. The artists, however, swore that they had rendered Moses and nobody else; they suggested that the fault lay with the experts in physiognomy. The king finally decided that there was only one way to settle his quandary: He would personally travel to the Sinai Desert and meet Moses.

When the king was granted an audience with Moses, with great hesitation he explained the purpose of his visit. Moses answered that indeed everything the experts in physiognomy had interpreted from the painting was so. These immoral traits were his congenital tendencies and dispositions. However, he had worked hard for many years to overcome those tendencies. He was capable of performing miracles and speaking "face to face" with God not because he was born perfect and righteous, but because he had mastered his own base traits through unremitting effort.

Roger Bannister was the "Moses" of running. Until May 6, 1954, it was considered impossible to run a mile in less than four minutes. On that day, Roger Bannister broke the four-minute record. Once he did it, others followed suit. Within the next year, Bannister's own record was broken. Moses was the Roger Bannister of spirituality. He set the record that all of us can now emulate.

Sure, we have cravings, desires, and temptations that seem to be an innate part of us. The secret is that those temptations are there for us to overcome. In so doing, we achieve greatness.

A famous Hasidic master, Rebbe Zusia of Anopoli, declared: "When I die and go to heaven, they will not ask me, 'Why were you not Moses?' They will ask me: 'Why were you not Zusia?' So I will answer, 'But I was Zusia.' And I will be told, 'Do you have any idea what the real Zusia was capable of? You were maybe a quarter of Zusia . . . maybe a half of Zusia.'"

Your potential is vast, even infinite, because it is rooted in your essential spiritual identity as "the image of God." The *real you* may very well be someone you've dreamed of, but thought incapable of actualizing. Or, it may be someone you've never dreamed of—at least, *not yet*.

In Hebrew, the word for human being is made up of the same letters as the Hebrew word for "very." This is because the essence of being human is to achieve superlative status. A human being must never stagnate or become complacent. A human being must be a "very," constantly striving to become better and greater. Being a human being means going beyond innate limitations. As Victorian poet Robert Browning wrote, "A man's reach should exceed his grasp or what's a heaven for."

One of my favorite writers, the late Aryeh Kaplan, was perhaps the greatest "spiritual marathoner" of recent times. Upon his death at 48, he had already published forty-eight books. Many of his other manuscripts have been published posthumously. Employing his dual brilliance as physicist and Torah scholar, Aryeh Kaplan was able to take the loftiest mystical subjects and make them comprehendible.

On the subject of actualizing one's potential, he wrote:

> We are living now in a time of breaking barriers. Everything that people always assumed to be impossible is becoming possible in our time. God may be teaching us a very important lesson with this: we are capable of doing things that we never thought possible. The paradigm of this is running a marathon race. If you ask anybody, "Can you run twenty six miles?" most people will give you an emphatic "No!" The truth is, however, that if we would spend enough time and really take it seriously, we could do it.

> The point is that the average person is capable of training himself to do something that is presently completely beyond his capacity. Furthermore, this is not limited to physical accomplishments. It is also true on an intellectual and spiritual level. Many people say, "I can't understand this; I will never be able to master this subject. This is too hard for me." If a person would really work at it, however, he or she could do anything. . . . By becoming a spiritual marathoner, a person could accomplish things that he would not dream possible.[123]

The very first creation mentioned in the Book of Genesis is light. "And God said, 'Let there be light.'" The verse then says that light and darkness were separated. Light was to be called "day" and darkness "night."

On the fourth day, the Torah tells us, the sun was created. Is this not an incredible conundrum? How can there be light without the sun? How can there be day and night without the earth's rotation in relation to the sun?

The light created on the first day of creation was a sublime spiritual

---

[123] *Inner Space* (Moznaim Publishing Corporation, New York, 1990) p. 167

energy, not physical light. When God separated light and darkness, night and day, He separated spirit from matter. Spiritual energy animates all of existence.

This design, of spirit empowering the physical, was to serve as a template for humanity. Temptations and cravings seem insurmountable only when the spirit is not taken into account. With the spirit, anything can be accomplished. The spiritual force in man can create, ennoble, enable, persevere, conquer, and survive the worst onslaughts, the basest cravings, the greatest dangers, and the most brutal conditions.

Let Someone Else Do It

If you are not in tip-top physical shape, the prospect of running a marathon can be daunting. All the effort, time, and sweat required to build up your endurance may not seem worth it. Similarly, although you may endorse the concept of a moral society, the prospect of adopting a higher moral standard for yourself may be daunting. "Let others actualize the ideal," you may say. "Society will not suffer from my one little indulgence."

A college fraternity once embarked on a fund-raising scheme. All 200 members of the fraternity were asked to contribute a cup of whiskey. The cups of whiskey would be poured into a vat. The full vat of whiskey would then be raffled off for five dollars a ticket. The lucky winner would be awarded the entire vat.

One member of the fraternity calculated that it really would not make a difference if he filled his cup with water and poured it into the vat. "After all," he rationalized, "there will be 199 other guys filling it with whiskey. No one will be able to detect my cupful of water." So this fraternity member poured a cup of water instead of whiskey into the vat.

The raffle took place with great fanfare. The winner was overjoyed. With the entire fraternity assembled, the president of the fraternity filled a shot glass from the vat and handed it to the winner, who downed it in one gulp. Everyone stood by, expecting him to grin with pleasure. Instead, he looked first surprised, then irate. "This is nothing by a vat of water!" he exclaimed angrily. All 199 other fraternity members had had the same idea of contributing water instead of whiskey; sure that it wouldn't make a difference.

What each individual in a society does makes a difference. "In the grand scheme of things," you may think, "my actions don't really count. I will leave it up to the rest of the citizens to maintain a high moral standard." The result is that too many people fill the vat of life with baseness instead of value. *It is up to you to save the world.*

It is an axiom of the Torah that the entire universe was created for the sake of man. All stars, angels, animals, and protozoa exist for the sake of man. The Torah charges every person to say to himself: "For me the world was created." This empowers, but also obligates.

It is your world. It is yours to keep sane. It is yours to keep safe. It is yours to keep clean. It is yours to keep holy. Don't leave this task up to others. Just as everyone's contribution builds the whole, so everyone's dereliction of duty destroys the whole.

A passenger on board a world-class cruise ship had a cabin on the bottom level. One day, he took out a drill from his valise and started drilling away at the wall of his cabin. His neighbor heard the noise and immediately reported it to the crew. In moments, the security officials charged into the cabin and demanded that he stop endangering the ship. The passenger responded that it was nobody's business but his own. It was his cabin, which he paid for, and he was entitled to do with it whatever he wished.[124]

In reality, each and every one of us is a passenger on the great ship called this world. Like the above passenger, we settle into our own cabins—our own independent existences. We too make decisions, which satisfy our own desires and drives, heedless of the effect of our actions on society as a whole.

We know that ecologically one miscreant can ruin an entire environment. One manufacturer who does not properly dispose of his toxic waste or one magnate in the Amazon region who decides to clear a few thousand acres of forest will negatively impact thousands of other people—for generations. The same is true morally. One person who acts in a debased manner negatively impacts the whole level of society. Decide right now that that person won't be you.

---

[124] These stories were based on the parables of R. Jacob Krantz, colloquially known as the "Dubno Maggid."

The Conundrum
of Suffering

Nineteen

Does God Get Away with Murder?

Is God Moral?

The book *If You Were God* gives us a "Mission Impossible" assignment. Here is your mission:

You become master of an island where several tribes live—different peoples from various ethnicities and backgrounds. By nature and culture, these tribes are exploitative and belligerent. This results in much suffering caused by war, poverty, and prejudice. They have been living this way for centuries without any sign of improvement.

Your assignment is to improve that society, to teach its members to live together in harmony and to reduce suffering to a minimum or eliminate it entirely. You must create a healthy society.

You are granted many resources, all the resources that a highly advanced technology can offer, in order to implement this assignment. You have been endowed with special powers so that you may control all aspects of life. You have the entire island under surveillance and can see what is happening in any place at any time. You have devices such as cloud-seeding equipment and can plant underground explosives. You can control weather, flooding, volcanoes and earthquakes, and produce any "natural" phenomenon on cue.

It is also within your power to implant ideas through subliminal suggestion. You can implant ideas to entire populations or to select leaders. In essence, you play God.

There are some restrictions to this game. Under no circumstances are the natives of this island to be aware of your presence. This supersedes all other considerations. The reason for this is simple. The cultural shock caused by your revealing yourself would disrupt the entire fabric of the island culture. It would cause much suffering and more than offset any good that you could possibly accomplish. The people would be reduced to a vegetable-like dependence from which they would be unlikely to recover. If they did recover, they might rebel so violently as to eliminate any positive values they might have originally gained. Therefore, the restriction that you not reveal yourself must be followed without exception, under any circumstance.[125]

An intriguing assignment! What would you do? It dawns on you that in order for a society to thrive even for a short length of time, some steadfast laws and principles must be established. Without rules, havoc would ensue. Corruption, promiscuity, vandalism, and disorder would permeate the society.

If you are indeed master over everything in this place, then you also control the inhabitants' thoughts and actions. What then prevents you from programming their minds to have no whims, desires, or compulsions for evil? People could be programmed to be kind, respectful, and law-abiding. It would be a utopian society, free of all evil.

This sounds like a great idea, one so good that you wonder why God didn't do likewise when He created the world.

We live one short generation after the Holocaust, which saw the brutal murder of six million Jews and millions of other Slavs, gypsies, and political undesirables. Other genocides have taken place and continue to take place in locations as far-flung as Cambodia and the Sudan. Innocent people suffer and despots thrive. Many people ask a legitimate question: Why does God allow innocent people to suffer? Why doesn't He stop the rampage of evil over good?

---

[125] This concept and many of the ideas mentioned in this chapter are adapted from *If You Were God* (NCSY, New York, 1995), a literary masterpiece by the master writer and scholar Aryeh Kaplan

In his classical work, *Guide to the Perplexed*, Maimonides explains that it is man, not God, who brings most evil to the world. Man, not God, makes wars. Man, not God, perpetrates genocide. Yet this does not answer the crux of the question. Granted, God does not perform the evil, but He does allow it to occur, and He did create the possibility of evil.

Let's restate the questions: Why does God allow evil to exist? Couldn't He have created a wholly good world? Couldn't God have made us totally moral?

The 18th century Jewish philosopher Moshe Chaim Luzzatto[126] explained that God wanted to confer upon his creations the ultimate good possible. *The ultimate good possible is God Himself.* There is no greater good than achieving a degree of unity with the Creator. But God did not want to humiliate humans by conferring this exalted state as a free gift, as charity. Therefore, God set up a system whereby humans could earn a high spiritual level of Divine closeness by choosing good over evil. Therefore, he endowed humans with free will and the responsibility to make choices.

God could have created a race of puppets or robots, devoid of the temptation toward evil, but then He could not have rewarded them for choosing good. Common sense dictates that in a world of only good, free will would serve little purpose. As Aryeh Kaplan explains, if nothing but good were possible, it would produce no benefit. As the Talmud puts it, "It would be like carrying a lamp in broad daylight."

The Zohar explains: "The advantage of wisdom comes from darkness. If there were no darkness, then light would not be discernible and would produce no benefit. This explains why God must conceal Himself from us."

Luzzatto goes a step further:[127]

> God created the forces of evil in this world—and allows them to
> temporarily overpower the good—in order to provide the good
> with an opportunity to summon forth its latent inner strength

---

[126] Rabbi Moses C. Luzzato (1707-1746), in his opus, *The Way of God* (Phillip Feldheim, New York, 1999)

[127] In his treatise *The Knowing Heart* (Phillip Feldheim, New York, 1982)

and ultimately obliterate evil. The triumph of the dark forces over those of light is always temporary, because the light is destined to burst out with hitherto untapped brilliance to wash away the stain of darkness.

Aryeh Kaplan explains that God's purpose does not allow man to exist in an intellectual prison. How would man behave if God were to constantly reveal Himself? Would he really be free? If man were constantly made aware that he was standing in God's presence, could he go against His will? Man's constant awareness of a manifest God would make him a prisoner. It would take away from his free will.

This likewise explains why there are no grand-scale open miracles today and why each time we sin, a bolt of lightning doesn't descend from the heavens and kill us. If God's presence were constantly manifest to us, we would live in perennial fear. We would scrupulously consider our every move. We would never sin or lose control. Life would lose its aspect of free choice and challenge. We would become automatons.

Is Suffering Random?

This doesn't mean that God doesn't punish us. According to the Talmud, God preordains every injury, even a finger prick.

Is there than absolutely nothing random that comes our way? Differentiating between which events that occur to us are random and which are Divine may be challenging. The Talmud sheds light on this with an interesting story about a noted Talmudic personality, Levi: [128]

> Due to a prolonged absence of rain, Levi proclaimed a fast for the populace. (Fasting and prayer was a way of entreating God to send rain.) Rain still did not come. Levi then said to God, "Master of the Universe! You went up and sat on high land. You do not have mercy on your children." God answered Levi's prayer and rain came, but Levi became lame because he had spoken disrespectfully to God.

---

[128]   Tractates Taanis, 25a; Sukka, 53a

The Talmud asks, "Was it this act of disrespect that caused Levi to become lame? Elsewhere we learned that Levi demonstrated *kiddah* bowing (an acrobatic form of prostrating oneself during prayer) in front of his master. In the process, he dislocated his hip and this is what caused him to become lame." Thus, this *kiddah* bowing made him lame, not his disrespect toward God. The Talmud resolves the matter: "Both this and that caused him to become lame."

Let us elucidate the Talmud's answer. As propounded above, God doesn't send instantaneous punishment to reprimand us. He did not immediately punish Levi for his disrespect. Instead, He waited for an occasion when Levi would place himself in a precarious position. Levi made himself vulnerable by his acrobatic stunt, but the injury occurred because of his disrespect toward God. This explains the Talmud's cryptic remark, "Both this and that caused him to become lame." The first action caused the punishment, but the second enabled its implementation.

Maimonides also discusses the subject of how God operates.[129] He writes that God set into motion the physical laws by which the world operates, such as gravity and magnetism. If a person were to take an apple and place it at the edge of his roof, the law of gravity would necessitate that the apple fall. Similarly, if someone stands on the edge of a roof and is pushed, gravity dictates that the person will fall down. These actions don't happen because God ordained it for a particular circumstance, but because they are general physical laws.

Similarly, if somebody puts himself in certain danger (e.g. he jumps out of an airplane), physical laws will negate his chances for survival. Or if somebody smokes or drinks dangerously, biological laws indicate that he will, in all probability, develop a fatal disease. However, if a person receives a blow that cannot be ascribed with 100% certainty to physical or biological laws, then he must attribute it to a personal encounter with God. So it is fair to estimate that for an average person with moderate to healthy habits, a large percentage of the incidents in his life are Divinely orchestrated.

God also established spiritual laws through which the universe

---

[129] In his introduction to Ethics of Our Fathers, *The Eight Chapters*

operates. Like the law of gravity, these spiritual laws also operate with 100% consistency. If a person disobeys spiritual laws, he endangers himself—just as if he were to jump off a skyscraper. The only difference is that the effect of a spiritual law may not be immediately apparent. This insures the preservation of the exercise of free will.

Spiritual laws are the directives of God, as expressed in the Torah. When these laws are challenged, serious danger to the soul ensues.

A common idiom is to refer to natural events as "Mother Nature." This idiom may be sacrilegious because God and nature are, to an extent, inseparable. I say "to an extent" because I wish to preclude any notion of Pantheism. God is not the world and God is not the force of nature; God is the Creator, Who dominates the world and Who controls the forces of nature.

God crafted the laws of nature during the process of creation. God's rules for nature included laws that allowed for nature to run a different or counter course at certain points in history. The most famous of these examples is the "splitting of sea," the manna falling from heaven, and all the miracles that the Children of Israel experienced in their exodus from Egypt.

Free Will and God's Ways

Let's get back to free will. If God's knowledge is infinite, this means that He knows exactly what kind of life each person will live: whether he will be good or bad, prosperous or poor. How does God's foreknowledge coexist with free will?

In his book, *Living Judaism*,[130] Dr. Paul Forchheimer addresses this question. He explains that while this conflict seems superficially insoluble, it can only arise out of the restricted nature of our imagination and vocabulary, which causes us to project features of human nature into our imperfect representation of the "qualities" of God. We have to realize that, although we apply the word "knowledge" to God, it does not and *cannot* mean what it means when applied to man.

Another problem arises when we analyze the Biblical account of

---

[130]   Phillip Feldheim, New York, 1983

the Egyptians enslaving the Israelites. As is stated in the book of Exodus, the Egyptians were punished for enslaving and persecuting the Israelites. However, in the book of Genesis God warns Abraham that the Egyptians will enslave his descendants for over four hundred years. It seems, then, that Pharaoh and the Egyptians were merely fulfilling a role that was preordained many years before. So, why were they held accountable? Additionally, this seems to contradict the entire thesis of free will that has so far been presented. How could God preordain the actions of the Egyptians and yet afford them free will?

In actuality, this question may be asked of all evil agents used by God to chastise His people. Pharaoh, Nebuchadnezzar, Haman, the Crusaders, Stalin, Hitler, Saddam Hussein, and Osama Bin Laden all chose evil and were accountable for their evil choices. However, in the grand scheme of history, they merely played roles already ordained by Divine decrees.

The answer to this conundrum is that God chooses evil people (i.e. people who have consistently chosen evil) in order to execute evil decrees. He takes people who are fixed in their ruthless and callous ways, and utilizes their evil for His Divine purposes. This is their punishment: *to further their evil.*

But what about a different scenario, when innocent parties are involved in causing harm? For example, if a driver hits a child who ran out into the street, is he also culpable?

The Talmud addresses this issue[131] in a section discussing the laws of murder. According to the Law, if it is proven beyond a shadow of a doubt that someone was guilty of premeditated murder, he receives capital punishment. If, however, someone kills another person inadvertently, by accident, with only minimal negligence, he is sentenced to exile in a "city of refuge," as prescribed in the Torah (Numbers 35:9-34). There he must stay for the rest of his life, or until the death of the High Priest.

Why should an innocent person be so confined? The Talmud explains that the fact that God caused bloodshed to come to his hand insinuates that he is not so innocent. As the Biblical verse states

---

[131] Tractate Makkos, 10b

(I Samuel 24:13), "From the wicked comes forth wickedness." God used a person who was already culpable as the agent for this "accidental" death.

The Talmud goes on to explain the case of two people. One was accused of murder, but the authorities lacked adequate witnesses. The second person had killed a person inadvertently, unbeknownst to anybody. Seemingly by chance, God arranges for these two people to come to the same inn. The one who killed intentionally sits under a ladder, while the other one descends the ladder, and accidentally falls upon him and kills him. The result of this chain of events is that the murderer is killed as he deserved, and the inadvertent killer is exiled, since he has now committed manslaughter in the presence of witnesses.

Justice is served on both counts, although to the bystanders it is a tragic accident. Such bystanders may feel it is unjust of God to allow the "innocent" person sitting under the ladder to be killed. They wonder how a just God could allow such an atrocity. This is exactly the lesson to be culled from this Talmudic teaching. *We mortals can't assume that we know the full picture, because usually we don't know even a fraction of the story.*

Let's return to Pharaoh. The Torah records that God repeatedly hardened the heart of Pharaoh, so that he refused to release the Israelites from bondage. If God alters a person's psyche and causes him to act in a certain way, isn't this a contradiction of free will?

One explanation is that Pharaoh suffered from extreme denial. He was so obsessed with enslaving the Jews that he turned a blind eye to all the plagues and manifestations of God's awesome power. In his *Eight Chapters,* Maimonides explains that this was exactly God's way of punishing Pharaoh. God allowed Pharaoh to follow the course that he himself had already chosen. He denied him the novel perception that may have changed his course.

Another principle is that in His conversation with Abraham, God did not implicate every individual Egyptian. He did not say that each Egyptian would persecute the Israelites. So each Egyptian was responsible for his actions, because any individual could have opted out of the general decree. Also, instead of merely enslaving the Jews, the Egyptians subjected them to torture, sadistic cruelty, and murder. Since this evil was their own choice, they deserved to be punished for it.

There are two approaches toward understanding God's knowledge in relation to human beings:

1) God's knowledge concerning eventual developments (i.e. changes occurring in individual personalities) is not the reason for their taking place. Rather, they develop due to their changeable nature. This means that God acts as a casual observer watching the events unfold. He doesn't tamper with any decisions that go into the process. So, His knowledge of events does not generate their eventual existence.

According to this approach, God's knowledge is somewhat comparable to asking a child to choose between an ice cream sundae and broccoli. The fact that you know almost definitively what the child will choose does not hinder the child's free will. It is also predictable that as the child matures his choices will mature accordingly.[132]

2) God does not "know" with a knowledge that is outside of Him such as humans know, because humans and their knowledge are two different entities. On the contrary, God and His knowledge are one and the same. Human knowledge of events assumes a time relation. Time is only a dimension of matter and is part of the physical universe. Genesis teaches that before the world was created there was nothing. We therefore cannot think what was "before" creation, as time exists only in the physical universe. We understand that God is independent of the physical universe. Therefore, time is

---

[132] Based on Saadya Gaon (882-942) in his work, *The Book of Beliefs and Opinion* (Yale University Press, New Haven, Connecticut, 1958), which is one of the earliest books dedicated to elucidating the fundamentals of Jewish philosophy and belief.

an irrelevant term applied to God. Therefore the question of His "previous" knowledge has no meaning with reference to absolute facts.[133] God exists in past, present and future—all simultaneously. So God isn't anticipating or orchestrating your future, because your future is God's present.[134]

The anonymous author of *The Disputation* sums up this approach brilliantly. He explains that the past has existed and exists in the future, as the relation of cause and effect, but the present has no true existence, as it is gone when we experience it. The only true present is the existence outside time, with God. To Him past and future are present.

We can better understand this concept if we imagine a subway line that traverses various avenues. Let's assume that these avenues are alphabetical and that the passenger's present location is Avenue "L," he departed from Avenue "B," and his destination is Avenue "R." While the passenger is at Avenue L, his "past" is Avenue B, while his "future" is Avenue R. He no longer has any contact with his past (Avenue B), and his future (Avenue R) is beyond him. Think however, about a helicopter pilot who is hovering above the subway line. It is quite possible that the helicopter pilot's view encompasses Avenues B, L, and R concurrently. In another words, the pilot sees the past, present and future of the subway passenger all at once. We are similar to the passenger, while God is like the helicopter pilot.

Nachmanides[135] explains that on "day one" of creation, time was created. Referring to Nachmanides' statement, Dr. Gerald Schroeder, formerly of M.I.T. and the U.S. Atomic Energy Commission, writes:[136]

> That's a phenomenal insight. Time was created. And that's exactly
> what Einstein taught us in the Laws of Relativity: that there was
> a creation, not just of space and matter, but of time itself. Albert

---

[133]   Aristotle writes along these lines in Physics VIII, 1.

[134]   This second theory is based on R. Joseph Albo (1210-1280) in his *Book of Principles*

[135]   (1194-1270) Gerona, Spain, in his commentary to the Bible

[136]   *Genesis and the Big Bang* (Bantam Books, 1991)

Einstein taught us that Big Bang cosmology brings not just space and matter into existence, but that time is part of the nitty gritty. Time is a dimension. Time is affected by your view of time.

As Dr. Forchheimer concludes, our mind is used to space-time surroundings to which we are familiar, and we cannot really think beyond them. But although unable to understand God, we can realize that He knows everything, yet that we have full moral liberty and, therefore, responsibility. That responsibility is augmented by the fact that God gave the Law to aid us in making the correct decisions.

Twenty

The Holocaust

According to the Bible, the Children of Israel are God's "chosen people." We might assume that this means that the Jewish people have been granted favored status, like a favorite child is indulged and pampered. History, however, reveals the opposite. Instead of being granted immunity, the Jewish nation has been the most persecuted people on earth. They have been subjected to massacres, crusades, inquisitions, holocausts, and expulsions from almost every country in Europe. Jewish survival in the face of such persecution is itself the most unlikely of miracles. Why have the Jews been subjected to such suffering?

I would like to preface my response to this question with a quote from Victor E. Frankl, a renowned psychiatrist and a survivor of the Holocaust:

> After a while I proceeded to another question, this time addressing myself to the whole group. The question was whether an ape that was being used to develop poliomyelitis serum— and for this reason punctured [by hypodermic needles] again and again—would ever be able to grasp the meaning of its suffering. Unanimously, the group replied that of course it would not; for with its limited intelligence it could not enter into the world of man, i.e. the only world in which its suffering would be

understandable. Then I pushed forward with the following question: And what about man? Are you sure that the human world is a terminal point in the evolution of the cosmos? Is it not conceivable that there is still another dimension possible, a world beyond man's world; a world in which the question of and ultimate meaning of human suffering would find an answer?"[137]

It may be impossible with our human, finite minds to ever come to terms with an event of such magnitude as the Holocaust. That said, I will discuss in this chapter theories that have been advanced to explain Jewish suffering in general and the Holocaust in particular.

One theory is that Jews suffer because of their collective failure to live up to the exalted standard of conduct required of them by the Torah. Although the Bible guarantees the immutable status of the Jews as God's chosen people, it also, in very explicit terms, threatens extreme punishment to the Jewish people for abandoning God's commandments. It also says that God will hide His countenance and allow terrible atrocities to occur.

As Professor Lawrence Kelemen wrote:

> The Bible makes clear that the Jewish people's covenant with God works in two directions. To the extent that the Jews differentiate themselves from all other peoples by observing God's commandments, God places them above normal historical processes and preserves them... When large segments of the Jewish people assimilate and leave their heritage behind, the Bible suggests, then the entire Jewish people will taste normality; then it will feel the pressure of that evolutionary force that drives people out of existence.[138]

According to historian Lucy S. Dawidowicz, Soviet Jewry aside, only about half of pre World War II Eastern European Jewry were observant, and "secularity was becoming the dominant mode."[139]

This seems unfair. After all, even if many or most of the Jewish nation sin, why should everyone, including the righteous members, suffer? The

---

[137] *Man's Search for Meaning* (Pocket Books, 1997)

[138] *Permission To Believe* (Tagum/Feldheim, New York, 1990) p. 85

[139] *The War Against the Jews 1933-1945* (Bantam Books, New York, 1975) p. 335

Maharal, the great 16th century mystic of Prague, explains that the Jewish people are not a mere collection of disparate individuals, but rather an integral unit, much like a human body. Because the body is one integrated organism, no matter which part of the body acts badly, the entire organism suffers. For example, if a diabetic eats too much sugar, would we expect that his digestive system, the "offending organ" would suffer? No, it is his feet that will be in danger of amputation! Or if a person who smokes suffers a heart attack, would we be surprised that the heart, rather than the hand that lifted the cigarette to the mouth, was afflicted? Of course not.

In the case of the Jewish people, this would mean that the entire nation, both righteous and evil, suffers when any part of the "organism" offends the Divine system with which the Jews have been charged.

In truth, the persecution to which the Jews have been subjected is not supernatural. The opposite is true. That the Jews, a tiny remnant of a nation exiled from its land for 2,000 years, has continued to survive bespeaks supernatural Divine protection. When the Jews sin, however, God simply withdraws His protective hand and allows them to be vulnerable to their enemies.

The most recent "large scale" tormentors of the Jewish nation have been the Nazis and Hamas, the Palestinian/Arab terrorist organization. In the Biblical account dealing with the mourning over the destruction of the Holy Temple and the mass slaughter of the Jews, the Hebrew word describing God's anger is *b'Natzi*. When the Torah wants to denote mass corruption by the people that leads to utter destruction it uses the term *Hamas*. Thus, the Nazis and Hamas are chilling reminders of human culpability that elicits fierce punishment.

When the Israelites were in the desert following their exodus from Egypt, God brought them to the borders of the Promised Land. There the people rebelled, refusing to enter the Land of Israel, and cried piteously about the supposed dangers of the Land. God ordained that the date on which the people had cried without cause, would become a day on which future generations would have ample cause to cry. That day was the ninth of the Hebrew month of *Av*.

This promise can serve as a litmus test for the Divinity of the Torah. Did any other significant events occur on that day throughout history? All of the following calamities occurred on the Ninth of Av:

1. The Babylonians, led by Nebuchadnezzar, destroyed the First Temple. 100,000 Jews were slaughtered and millions more exiled. (586 BCE)
2. The Romans, led by Titus, destroyed the Second Temple. Some two million Jews died, and another one million were exiled. (70 CE)
3. The Bar Kochba revolt was crushed by the Roman Emperor Hadrian. The city of Betar—the Jews' last stand against the Romans—was captured and liquidated. Over 100,000 Jews were slaughtered. (135 CE)
4. The Temple area and its surroundings were plowed under by the Roman general Turnus Rufus. Jerusalem was rebuilt as a pagan city—renamed Aelia Capitolina—and access was forbidden to Jews.
5. Pope Urban II declared the first Crusade. (1095)
6. King Edward I signed the edict compelling the Jews to leave England. (1290)
7. The Jews were expelled from Spain. (1492)
8. World War I broke out in 1914 when Germany declared war on Russia. German resentment from this war set the stage for the Holocaust.
9. The Arabs began their riots in the city of Jerusalem. (1929)
10. The mass deportation of Jews from the Warsaw Ghetto, en route to Treblinka, began. (1942)

There are no coincidences. Jewish suffering is Divinely ordained, and perhaps comes in response to the failure of some/many Jews to live up to their Divine mission.

The Antecedents of the Holocaust

The question, which challenges the present, post-Holocaust generation more than perhaps, any other is: How can a just and moral God have allowed the Holocaust?

If one accepts the principle of Divine punishment for failure to obey the Torah's injunctions, then even a cursory glance at pre-War World II Jewish life would cast this question in a different light. In the monumental book *The Disputation,* it is stated that as a result of the French Revolution and the Napoleonic Wars, freedom and the spirit of liberalism triumphed in Europe. The ghettos of Germany were opened and, for the first time in centuries, Jews took their place as free men and equal citizens. The genius which had turned inward now turned outward, and, instead of being concentrated on the Torah, spent itself on medicine, philosophy, science, music, art, finance, industry and politics. Everywhere it flowered. The Jews started to assimilate. What centuries of oppression and torture could not do a few decades of freedom did. Except for an obstinate and sturdy core, the bulk of European Jewry Christianized.

In the mid-nineteenth century, a neo-Jewish movement began in Berlin, Germany. This movement claimed that the holy Torah had not been God-given, and therefore was not incumbent on Jews to follow. According to their views, the Torah was a man-made document subject to change and, in "modern times," obsolete. In 1837, Abraham Geiger called the first Reform rabbinical conference in Weisbaden, Germany, and declared: "The Talmud must go, the Bible, that collection of mostly so beautiful and exalted human books, as a divine work must also go."[140]

Samuel Holdheim eventually headed the Reform congregation in Berlin. He disavowed many of the cardinal features of Judaism: circumcision, covered heads during worship, the prayer shawl, the blowing of the Shofar, the use of the Hebrew language, and the mention of Zion, Jerusalem, or the land of Israel in any of the services. According to Holdheim and his colleagues, "We know of no fatherland except that to which we belong by birth or citizenship."

By the middle of the nineteenth century, Reform had dethroned Jerusalem in favor of Berlin. The Jewish Sabbath was changed from Saturday to the Christian Sunday. The synagogue began resembling the church in its aesthetics and services. German Reform also had the gall to abolish the "automatic assumption of solidarity with Jews everywhere." Adherents of Reform described themselves as "Germans of the Mosaic persuasion," rather than as Jews.

This movement picked up momentum. Traditional observance by European Jewry gave way to assimilation, intermarriage, and conversion to Christianity. By the advent of the Holocaust, over 40% of German

---

[140]   Michael A. Meyer, *Response to Modernity: A History of the Reform Movement in Judaism* (New York: Oxford University Press, 1988), p. 91

Jews had intermarried. Even in Poland, that bastion of traditional Jewish observance, two-thirds of the Jewish population had ceased to keep the Sabbath. Thus, major portions of European Jewry by their own choice forfeited the miraculous Divine protection that shielded them from their enemies.

The theologians who endorse this explanation for the Holocaust point to the Divine curses that fill entire sections of Leviticus and Deuteronomy, threatening unspeakable punishments if the Jews abandon their Divine mission.

The Battle of Good and Evil

Another explanation for the Holocaust involves the eternal battle between good and evil. Hitler himself cast the war in these terms:

> It is true we Germans are barbarians; that is an honored title to us. I free humanity from the shackles of the soul: from the degrading suffering caused by the false vision called conscience and ethics. The Jews have inflicted two wounds on mankind: circumcision on its body and conscience on its soul. They are Jewish inventions. The war for the domination of the world is waged only between these two camps alone, the Germans and the Jews. Everything else is but deception.

In the following two chapters, I will explore the concept of suffering even more deeply, and hopefully shed more light on the inner workings beneath the tragedy of the Holocaust.

Can There Be Love of God after the Holocaust?

Whatever reasons God may have had to permit the Germans and other Europeans to perpetrate the Holocaust, how could God expect survivors of the Holocaust to still believe in Him, let alone love Him?

In an attempt to answer this question, I would like to consider two POW's of the Persian Gulf War. Royal Air Force pilot John Peters and his navigator John Nichol were sealed in their fighter-bomber, flying to a target deep in Iraq, when ground fire downed their plane. The British fliers were taken captive by Iraqi ground forces, who tortured them in a dire effort to extract as much damning information as possible for the war effort against the Allies.

Here is John Peters' account of his captivity:[141]

> A pack of guards dragged me into a room. Then they jumped me. It was a low-tech beating—just boots and fists. They grabbed my hair and threw my head against the wall. I fell. When they lifted me up I doubled over, twisting away from the blows. But with my hands cuffed behind my back, my front was wide open. The only sounds in the room were the scuffling of boots as the guards maneuvered to hit me . . . the sharp thwack and thud of flesh being hit . . . Even blindfolded I could distinguish the instruments of torture they were now using: a thick rubber strap across my face inflicted a penetrating sting; a wooden bat sent a jarring shock that went through to the bone . . .

Here is what John Nichol experienced:

> The first fist in my mouth was a mind-numbing shock. They crowded around me, whipping, kicking, punching, blows driven in from all angles. My bones felt crunched under the impact of the thudding boots . . . Finally they dragged me to another room, blindfolded me and stood me with my forehead flat against the wall, my feet about 20 inches away from it. I was stretched onto my toes, arms handcuffed behind my back. My forehead was supporting my entire body weight. Every time I tried to move, somebody punched me. The manacles on my arms were at the tightest notch. . . . In the evening they hauled me back to the interrogation center. "What squadron are you from?"
>
> "I cannot answer that . . ."

---

[141] From the book *Tornado Down* (published by Michael Joseph, London, U.K., 1992)

Bang! Somebody punched me. Blood came pouring out of my
face.

Question again: "I cannot . . ."

Thwack! Somebody hit me hard across the skull with a piece of
wood . . . Then somebody stuffed tissue paper down the back of
my T-shirt and set fire to the paper. I threw my head violently
from side to side to try to escape the burning . . .

The pilot and navigator were prepared to suffer terrible torture in
order to protect the interests of the Allies. Why? What can motivate a
person to endure such immense pain rather than simply spout out the
information the torturers are intent on extracting? Apparently, their
mission—and the integrity of their loyalty to it—was more important
to them *than their own lives.*

Let us now delve into this question: Whom do you think the POWs
directed their hatred towards? Did they hate the British Government,
who sent them on a mission that ended up exposing them to such
terrible torture, or the Iraqis?

Obviously, the answer is that they hated the Iraqis. They knew that
they were representing their government in a noble battle of good
against evil. This empowered them to pay the price for being the agents
of good.

We can draw a strong parallel between the POWs' amazing
resistance and self-sacrifice and the Jews of the Holocaust. Those Jews
who understood that they were representing God in a battle between
good and evil did not direct their abhorrence toward God but rather
toward the Nazis, who represented and personified evil. Such Jews
realized that relinquishing their faith meant succumbing to the evil of
the Nazis. These Jews knew that their supreme mission in this world
was to fight for God's sovereignty, even at the expense of their own
lives.

Twenty-One

Why Do Bad Things Happen?

The prophet Elijah once visited the celebrated Talmudic sage Rabbi Joshua. The rabbi entreated Elijah to allow him to accompany him on one of his incognito journeys. Elijah refused Rabbi Joshua's plea, but Rabbi Joshua continued imploring until Elijah reluctantly consented—but on one condition: Under no circumstances was Rabbi Joshua to question his actions. If he did, Elijah would leave him on the spot. The rabbi agreed, and they set forth.

Their first visit was to a poor, elderly couple. This couple lived in an impoverished hut, with nothing but two simple cots. Their only source of sustenance was a thin cow. The couple graciously received the two anonymous visitors. They offered them the only food they had, milk, and insisted that the guests sleep in their beds while they slept on the floor. In the morning, Rabbi Joshua heard Elijah pray that this couple's cow should die. A few minutes later, the distraught husband came running into the hut, crying that their cow had died. Rabbi Joshua was appalled, but he had to keep silent.

Next they went to a wealthy man who was in the process of building himself a mansion. The wealthy man had no time for the travelers, nor did he offer them any food, nor a place to sleep. Lying on the hard ground outside the building site, Rabbi Joshua heard Elijah pray that God should send angels to hastily finish the construction of the mansion.

Rabbi Joshua could no longer restrain himself. He asked Elijah to explain why he had rewarded the wicked man and punished the righteous couple. Elijah agreed to explain, although immediately afterward Rabbi Joshua must leave him. Elijah explained that the righteous elderly woman had been ordained to die that night. Moved by her kindness, Elijah begged God to allow the cow to die in her place. Regarding the wealthy man, Elijah had seen that he was on the verge of discovering a huge buried treasure in the process of his construction. Elijah prayed that the construction be completed by angels, so that the treasure would remain hidden.

In each case, what looked to the observer as callous and unfair was actually just and kind. So it is with all recompense in this world. Only God can see the entire picture, including what might have been. Therefore, all human judgments of "fair" and "unfair" are necessarily based on insufficient evidence.

A great rabbi, Elchonon Wasserman, provided deep insight into the issue of Divine justice just before the Nazis murdered him and his entire family, save for one son. In an effort to explain the extermination of the Jews, Rabbi Wasserman told this parable:

A man who had spent his entire life living in the city moved to a farm. He stood and observed a field next to his rented quarters. The field was so perfect and smooth, with green grass covering it like a blanket. Suddenly he saw a farmer with a menacing tool begin to cut ridges into the field and to turn over the sod. The city dweller looked on in dismay as the farmer seemingly ruined his field by plowing it. He continued to watch. Now the farmer took what appeared to be perfect seeds and stuck them into the dirt. Next, the farmer took precious water and deliberately poured it over the soil, making the soil muddy.

The city spectator continued his observation for several weeks. To his great surprise, he saw green shoots sprout from the soil. Soon the sprouts grew to full-fledged stalks of wheat. With the curious city dweller following in tow, the farmer harvested his grain and took it to a mill. The city dweller looked on aghast as the farmer poured his perfectly good grain into a machine, which decimated it, grinding it to powder. Then the farmer took this powder, the meager produce of all his labor, to the kitchen, where he mixed it with water and other ingredients. Before the observer could object, the seemingly demented farmer put his powdered grain into the fire to be burned. The city dweller had to be restrained from hitting the farmer over the head and turning off the oven. A short while later, he saw the farmer open the oven and remove an impressive, perfect loaf of bread. From all that seeming destruction came a beautiful finished product.

According to Rabbi Wasserman, we are similar to the city dweller when we look with our finite eyes at unfolding events. Sometimes we judge God's actions as callous and cruel only because we do not have the ability to see the final product.

The Body Takes the Brunt

At times our bodies have to suffer for the good of our souls. God designed us in such a way that the physical body is subsidiary to the soul. While a person may believe that he is living for the sake of his body, he is in actuality living for the sake of his soul. The objective of life is to perfect the soul so that the soul can return to its Maker in holiness and purity.

Medical science gives us a glimpse into how God works. When virulent bacteria invade a body, they thrive precisely at the body's normal temperature of 98.6 degrees. Once these bacteria take up residence in the human body, they proliferate exponentially. The body's immune system mounts a defense, but cellular defenders may be thwarted or overwhelmed. So the body is in trouble. Salvation comes from a mechanism that the average person views as a foe. A furnace is turned up in the body. The body suffers and cringes from the heat, and takes Tylenol to get rid of that accursed fever. Fever, however, actually fights the bacteria. Acutely sensitive to the temperature increase, the pathogens perish. Then the fever breaks, and the patient gets well.

Sometimes the soul is sick. Various foreign entities have invaded and are posing as lethal threats to the soul's purity and homeostasis.

So, "the furnace" is turned on, causing pain and suffering. This suffering may actually be the greatest healing agent for the soul.

The human soul, *the real you,* is literally a part of God. Having emanated from such glory, *the real you* comes to earth as a reflection of God's perfection. Then it is enclosed in a body of flesh and blood. It now becomes affected by man's physical limitations, and its vision of God's glory dims. This concealment is part of God's plan. If man—by his own efforts in climbing the ladder of spirituality—tears himself loose from the shackles of his earthly limitation and imperfection, he once more attains the revelation of God's oneness, and is reunited with Him.[142]

High-quality cars are built with internal frames. If the car is involved in a collision, the frame takes the beating while the driver may emerge intact. Inferior built cars, on the other hand, fold up like an accordion when they suffer the impact of a bad collision. Your body is like a Lexus protecting your soul, the driver. The body absorbs the damage of the collision so that your soul—*the real you*—may emerge unscathed.

By a law of spiritual physics, every action engenders "an equal and opposite reaction," so that every misdeed must cause suffering to the agent of the misdeed. That suffering can be experienced here in this world by the physical body, or in the next world. Since there is no physicality in the next world, there suffering can be experienced only by the soul. If a person doesn't receive punishment in this world, their soul, *their true self,* suffers in the World-to-Come. Therefore, it is in the human being's best interest to bear punishment for even the slightest infraction in this world, so that he may arrive in the next world free of blemish. The Talmud makes this point vividly clear when it says, "the suffering of the body cleanses a person of his sins."

Remember our analogy about the astronaut and the space suit? Let's take that analogy one step further. The astronaut is outfitted in his space suit and shipped to space for only a brief interval of time. The astronaut's goal is to spend this limited time in space productively— collecting data and enacting experiments. After accomplishing his

---

[142] As explained by Luzzatto, as well as elucidated by the founder of Habad Hassidism, Shneyur Zalman of Liadi, author of Tanya, as interpreted by Rabbi M. Munk

mission, the astronaut returns to earth, where he is divested of his space suit.

I would now like to share with you an idea that is so essential to understanding life that it may be the most paramount idea in this book: The world that we live in is not the *principle world*. Our world is a laboratory for human beings—for a limited period of time. The Talmud calls our world a "corridor" to the ultimate world.

Our world is then similar to space in the analogy recounted above. Just like the astronaut enters space for a limited time in order to accomplish great things, the human being enters this world from a higher, spiritual world to do the same. Similar to the astronaut being outfitted in the space suit prior to entering space, our souls, before making their debut into the physical world, are invested with physical bodies. The new composition, this fusion of physical body and soul, is what we call the human being. The human being spends limited time on planet Earth accomplishing various tasks. When the time comes for the human being to complete its earthly mission and return to the spiritual world, it must first be divested of its physical body, just as the astronaut removes his space suit when re-entering earth.

A parable offered by Rabbi Israel Meir Kagan (1828-1933), the towering codifier, ethicist and sage of his generation, makes this idea clear. A sailor becomes shipwrecked on an island. He is left naked and bare. The people of the island quickly robe him in splendid garments and take him to a palace. He is treated royally. Whatever he desires, he receives. He amasses a fortune of jewels and money.

Finally, some three months later, he begins to wonder why he is receiving such royal treatment. He decides to entrust his query to a royal advisor.

The advisor answers, "Really, you are the first person to be shipwrecked on our island who has asked this question. Everyone else figured, 'Why make trouble and start asking questions? Enjoy and be merry!' Officially, I am forbidden to divulge the answer to you. But we will keep it a secret. Every year we find somebody who was washed ashore from a shipwreck. He arrives, like you did, naked and empty-handed. We treat him royally for one year. As soon as twelve months are up, we take him back to the seashore, disrobe him, and send him back the way he arrived. All the wealth and jewels that he amassed stay behind. If I were you, I would take all the wealth that is being showered upon you and secretly send it away on different boats for storage when your year is up. This way, when you leave the island, you will leave laden with fortune."

The lesson, says Rabbi Kagan, is clear. When a person is born into this world, he arrives stark naked. Oddly, he is taken to a home and cuddled and loved, robed and fed. He is treated first-class. He is given every opportunity to amass fortunes. Does he ever stop to ask, "Why? Why am I getting such special treatment? What is the ultimate point to this all?" One day, maybe even abruptly, he is taken from this world and must leave everything behind. He goes as he arrived, naked and empty-handed. However, he *can* store away, just as the sailor was advised to do, not wealth and jewels, as that will have zero value when he meets his Creator. As the Talmud says, "Upon a person's death, not money, gold, precious stones nor jewels escort him to his grave. Only Torah study and good deeds accompany him."[143] He can store away the good deeds that he has accrued and acts of charity that he has performed. He then returns to his native place with real treasure.

Illness and the Healer

Job, a famous Biblical character, was an extremely righteous man. He was wealthy and was blessed with many devoted children. One day, God said to Satan, "Have you observed my servant, Job? Isn't he amazing? I can't find any fault in him."

Satan, being the cunning prosecutor that he was, claimed that Job had every reason to be pious. After all, he had it so good! The Satan argued that if God would deal Job a mortal blow, he would surely deny God. God had confidence in Job's faithfulness and awarded Satan the opportunity to test him.

So Satan got to work. Job was dealt really heavy blows. First his cattle died, then his children, then Job himself was afflicted with severe boils that left him in excruciating pain. Throughout all his suffering,

---

[143]   In Tractate Avot, Chapter 6:9

Job maintained his faith. In the end, all his affliction was removed from him, and he was rewarded several-fold.

Job had no way of knowing that all his anguish was temporary and for his own benefit. Yet, by growing in his faithfulness to God, Job grew as a human being.

Concerning illness and disease, God says,[144] "All the diseases that I placed on Egypt, I will not place on you [if you observe the Law]. I am God your Healer."

This is a perplexing statement. First, God says that He will not give us sickness and disease at all. Then he says that He is our Healer, implying that we might get sick. Why this ambiguity?

The classical commentator *Rashi* comments that even if God decides to inflict diseases it will be like He didn't, *because* He is the healer. R. Jacob of Lisa[145] explains: A surgeon, when healing a patient from disease or injury, excises skin or an organ in order to heal the damaged area. Even though tissue is being cut, one won't accuse the doctor of injuring the patient. He is doing something remedial. A dentist must sometimes cause the patient a lot of pain—but it is ultimately for the patient's welfare.

King Solomon said this very aptly;[146] "The wounds inflicted by a friend are trustworthy, while the kisses of an enemy are deceitful."

When a person suffers a "wound" at the hand of a friend, he may trust that the wound was intended for his benefit. By the same token, when he receives "kisses" from his enemy, he may assume that they are merely a ploy to deceive and harm him.

Imagine you are crossing the street when your friend forcefully knocks you to the ground. He knocked you down because a car was about to hit you. On the other hand, when the Patriarch Jacob went to the home of Laban, he was embraced and kissed by Laban. Laban was two-faced and cruel. He saw that Jacob, a very wealthy individual, came with no money or jewels. So he kissed him, thinking that he might find jewels stashed in his mouth.

When God sent the plagues to the Egyptians, He was serving them

[144] Exodus, 15:26

[145] R. Jacob Loerberbaum of Lisa (d. 1832)

[146] Proverbs, 27:6

long over-due punishment. They would never recuperate from this punishment. This type of injury God will not inflict upon His faithful. As He says, "All the diseases that I placed on Egypt, I will not place on you." God says that he will give us the type of injuries that a doctor would perform: "curative injuries"—afflictions that will serve to atone for the person or spur him on to repentance. And for such types of afflictions, "I am God your Healer."

As we confront enigmas in life that perplex us we must realize that our Creator, Who knows all, operates with knowledge of infinite breadth. Our minuscule minds can never comprehend the actions of God. Faith means that we realize that whatever God does is for the best, even though we may have difficulty in perceiving it as such. The secret to living a calmer life with less grievances is to develop a resolute faith in God and to realize that He knows better than we, and that all He does is for our ultimate good.

Bashert

"*Bashert*" is a word that I think should be added to our every day lexicon. *Bashert* is a Yiddish word, which means "meant to be." *Bashert* means that any event that transpires in life is intended for a reason. There is no such thing as a random event. Emotionally, the person who lives a life espousing the "*bashert* philosophy" fares better than others do. She has a way of coping with hurts and disappointments that might otherwise seem insurmountable.

Rabbi Akiva, one of the greatest Talmudic scholars, instituted the aphorism, "Whatever God does is for the good." It happened that his faith in this dictum was put to the test. Once he was in the middle of a journey and arrived at a town bordering a forest. He asked the townspeople for hospitality, but they refused. So he was forced to spend the night in the forest.

Rabbi Akiva was riding a donkey and had a lantern so that he could study at night and a rooster to wake him in the morning. A wind blew out the lantern's flame. A cat came and ate the rooster. A lion came and killed the donkey. He had nothing left. But Rabbi Akiva declared, "Whatever God does is for the good."

The next morning, as he approached the town, he heard cries and moans. He found out that the previous night, thugs had come to the town from the forest. They plundered, murdered, and injured everyone they found.

It now became profoundly clear to Rabbi Akiva why God had caused events to enfold as they had. Had he been invited to stay in the town for the night, he may have been murdered. Had the wind not blown out the lantern, the thugs would have seen him. Had the rooster and donkey remained alive, their crowing and braying would have alerted the bandits to Rabbi Akiva's vulnerable presence in the forest. Everything that had happened to him indeed was for the good.

God's Law teaches us to have faith that everything that occurs to us is for our ultimate good. No matter how negative a situation may seem, it occurs to steer us in a positive direction.

In his memoir, *Climbing the Mountain*, legendary actor, Kirk Douglas tells how he was once eager to get a role in a certain movie. He felt that he was perfect for the part. He was sure that the movie would be a tremendous success, and would even get an Oscar. Mr. Douglas desperately sought this role, but he was refused the part. In desperation, he prayed that God grant him the opportunity to play that role. When a colleague was chosen for the part, Mr. Douglas was extremely bitter. He couldn't understand why this had happened to him. He was upset at everyone connected with the film, and angry with God for not answering his prayers.

Just before the movie was released, Mr. Douglas saw a preview showing. He was extremely disappointed, and realized that the movie was a flop. He thanked God for having done what was best for him. He realized that instead of being bitter at those who hadn't given him the part, he should be thankful to them for being God's messengers in sparing him an embarrassing setback.

This is an integral concept in religion. The Bible commands us not to take revenge even if we were wronged or hurt. This seems to go against what is fair, and contradicts the human impulse to "get even."

One may not take revenge because one does not know why something has occurred. Was the guilty person acting purely on his own volition, or was his action, even unbeknownst to him, *"bashert"*—meant to be?

A man met a woman and they fell insanely in love. He built castles in the sky imagining their ultimate marriage. After a lengthy relationship, the woman of his dreams suddenly rejected him and went off with another man. He ended up marrying a different woman. Years later he found out that his first love was actually a convict fleeing from the law. It was the greatest blessing for him that his relationship with her was terminated.

This is why we are warned against taking revenge. Because we are mortals, we cannot fathom why people act as they do, nor how their actions will affect us in the long run. What looks like something unjust may actually be *just right*—in the grand scheme of things.

Even sickness or death can be *"bashert."* Many times sickness or tragedy catapults a person to do good or to spearhead innovative programs to save others. Countless lives have been saved and touched because of organizations such as M.A.D.D. (Mothers Against Drunk Driving) or the Make a Wish Foundation. Both these organizations were founded and are staffed by people who suffered the loss of their loved ones. But, again, viewing life with such a lens is challenging, because we understand things only as they appear in the present. For this reason, the Talmud prescribes different blessings for good and for bad. In blessing God, we acknowledge that we trust His actions even though we can't immediately fathom them. [147]

---

[147]   Talmud, Berachos 54a

Twenty-Two

Reincarnation

T he great Moses was very troubled by human suffering. Remember that from his perch in Pharaoh's palace, the young Moses witnessed the torture and affliction of enslaved human beings. According to some scholarly opinions, Moses' obsession with suffering prompted him to become the anonymous author of the Book of Job, the Bible's only direct exploration of the issue of why the righteous suffer. The Torah itself records that Moses implored God, "Show me, I pray, your Glory."[148] The commentators explain that this was Moses' request to understand God's ways, particularly why God permits suffering, injury, disease, death at an early age, afflicted children, etc.

God refused Moses' request. Maimonides explains why: "This was impossible since his intellect was bound to matter; that is to say, he was a human being. God therefore said to him: 'For man shall not see me and live.'"[149]

As Trude Weiss-Rosemarin wrote, "When Moses presumed to invade the eternal enigma of the Divine he was rejected and assigned to his own sphere, the sphere of all mortals."[150]

---

[148] Exodus, 33:18

[149] Exodus, 33:20

[150] *Judaism and Christianity: The Differences* The Jewish Book Club (1947)

According to the Midrash, God *did* provide Moses with a glimpse of the Divine. God showed Moses the following vision: A prince was galloping by a river. Seeing the refreshing water, he disembarked from his horse in order to drink, and accidentally dropped a purse of money. After his drink, he continued along his way.

Moments later, a young lad, who together with his mother was enslaved to an evil despot, happened to pass by that same spot. He chanced upon the purse and found a fortune of money. The boy ran back to his master's estate and redeemed himself and his mother. He then purchased a field that would sustain them for the rest of their lives.

A bit later an elderly man with a cane in hand came walking by the same river. After drinking some cool water, he lay down and went to sleep. In the meantime, the prince discovered that his precious purse was missing. He realized that it must have fallen out by the river when he bent over to drink, so he returned to the spot. The only person he found there was a sleeping elderly man. Try as he might, the prince couldn't find the purse. He figured that the elderly man had taken it and hidden it. So, he roused the old man from his sleep and demanded his money. The old man swore that he knew nothing of the purse. The prince didn't believe him, and killed him.

Moses was astounded. Where was equity in this vision? How could God allow such injustice? Why should the old man have been killed? Why did the prince lose his money? What merit did that child have to strike such good fortune?

God showed Moses another vision: A child and his father were returning home from years of labor. They had amassed a small fortune, and were so happy. Suddenly, out of the clear blue, an older man brandishing a sword appeared. He killed the father and took the money. A wealthy prince standing there witnessed the crime, but did nothing to prevent it.

God explained to Moses that the older man in the first story, who seemed to have been innocent, was a reincarnation of the man who killed the father and stole the money in the second story. The child who found the money in the first story was the same child, reincarnated, who had his money stolen in the second story. The prince, who in the second story was negligent in protecting the father and son, was reincarnated and penalized by losing his money. He also reappeared in the first story to slay the old man, whom he should have slain when the father and son were under attack.

Moses then understood that God's justice is impeccable.

As a contemporary scholar wrote in his commentary to Psalms:[151]

> It is both unreasonable and unwise to pass judgment on a work of art before it has been completed; even a masterpiece may look like a grotesque mass of strokes and colors, prior to its completion. Human history is God's masterpiece. Physical creation was completed at the end of the sixth day, but the spiritual development of mankind will continue until the world ends, at the close of the sixth millennium. Thus it is both unfair and impossible to judge God's equity before the denouement of human history, despite the fact that history appears to be a long series of human injustices.

Begging for Another Chance

Rabbi I. M. Kagan, one of the leading sages of the 20th century, masterfully addressed the question of human suffering by invoking the explanation of reincarnation, called in Kabbalah *gilgul neshamos,* meaning "recycling of souls."

To give a brief explanation of this Jewish concept: Kabbalah teaches that man is composed of body and soul. The *neshama*, or soul, makes us capable of spiritual and Godly pursuits. Humans were originally intended to live forever. After Adam's sin, humans were ordained to die. Had humans lived forever, they would have had an unlimited opportunity to correct their sins. Once death was introduced, humans faced a new predicament: They could die without repenting or redressing their sins. The *neshama* can't return to the Creator tarnished with sin, so it is doomed to remain in less desirable planes of existence.

The soul then begs to be given another chance. It asks to return to

---

[151] A.C. Feuer in his commentary to Psalm 92, *Tehillim* (Mesorah Publications, New York, 1991)

the world, in whatever form, to correct the mistakes that it had made. Sometimes God consents to the soul's wish and gives it this second opportunity. It is even possible for an entire generation to be sent back into this world to correct sins.

Rabbi Kagan addressed the topic of why it seems that good people suffer while the wicked prosper. Here is my modern-day adaptation of his words: Imagine that a physical body expires and its *neshama* goes to heaven. The *neshama* is judged by the heavenly court to ascertain what kind of life the person led. She will not be able to deny any of her actions because every second of her life is displayed on DVD, with precision accuracy. The prosecutors bring up a list of terribly serious charges, the worst of which are sins committed against her fellow humans. In this particular case, the woman was overly harsh and judgmental towards a disabled man. She scorned him and treated him without any pity. The *neshama* is now condemned to suffer for her sins by experiencing remorse that burns like the fires of hell. The soul shudders at the prospect and beseeches the heavenly court to reconsider its verdict.

Then she comes up with an alternative means to redress her sin. If God would send her into a body that was disabled, she would become sensitive to the plight of such people, and she would sincerely regret her sin, and thus attain *tikkun,* or repair. God tells the *neshama* that He will not subject her to the pain and anguish of being born physically disabled. It would be too harsh. The *neshama,* however, begs God to do so. Eventually, God consents, and the *neshama* is sent down to a disabled fetus in the womb and given another chance to repair its sin. The parents who must raise this child are likewise in need of rectification for some sin of a previous incarnation.

Mystical Meanings

Where is this concept alluded to in the Torah?

There are many obscure passages in the Torah. Let's examine one instance. The Bible commands, "You should not cook a goat in its mother's milk." [152]

---

[152] Exodus, 23:19, 34:26, Deuteronomy 14:21

This verse is mentioned three times in the Bible, and three derivations are deduced from it: a prohibition against eating milk and meat in the same meal, a prohibition to cook milk and meat together, and a prohibition against benefiting from a mixture of milk and meat.

The Midrash records that Moses asked God why He did not command these prohibitions in a straightforward way, e.g. "Thou shall not eat or cook meat and milk together, nor derive any benefit from this mixture." Moses pleaded with God to write these commandments explicitly. God explained to Moses that there were deep, mystical meanings that were encoded into these exact words. God stresses this by repeating the same commandment three individual times.

Another instance where the Torah verse has an abstract connotation is apropos the subject of reincarnation. The Torah states, "When a man gives a wound to his fellow, like he perpetrated against this man, so will be done to him: An eye for an eye. A tooth for a tooth . . ." [153]

The Talmud, in detail, proves that the Torah is not to be understood literally. The Torah does not mean that someone who knocks out another's eye should have his own eye knocked out; rather, it refers to the value of an eye, which the attacker must pay. But why the ambiguity? Why doesn't the verse simply state "the value of an eye for an eye"?

We explained previously that deep secrets are encrypted in such ambiguous verses. Indeed, the Kabbalists explain that the word used to describe the event in which "so will be done to him," is a future-tense word denoting a future event, which will be done by God Himself. In other words, God will exact measure for measure retribution in a future incarnation. If someone is guilty of injuring another person's limb, that person will suffer the same exact disability in a future incarnation.

In this world, however, human justice mandates only monetary compensation. The financial award is intended to appease the sufferer, but doesn't atone for the evil perpetrated. Divine retribution may take place in the person's present body or in a reincarnation in another body.

As explained previously, the *neshama* actually considers it a kindness to be reborn with the disability that she caused. This concept

---

[153]   Leviticus, 24:19

of kindness in relationship to reincarnation is actually hinted to in the Hebrew of these words. *Chesed*, the Hebrew word for kindness, has the same numerical value as *gilgul*, the Hebrew word for reincarnation.

The concept of reincarnation isn't confined to rectifying sins between man and man; it can also afford an opportunity to rectify sins that a person committed against God. For example, a person who wallowed in sexual immorality may be reborn into a body that is plagued with inordinate sexual temptations. While the person may feel that these strong temptations must be assuaged, the opposite may be true: the person may experience these strong inclinations only so that he will overcome them in this lifetime, and thus repair the sins of his previous incarnations.

Whether one's temptation is toward anger, laziness, addiction, illicit desire or any other moral failing, a person must make tremendous effort to overcome these temptations and thus effect a rectification (*tikkun*) for his soul. The Talmud[154] prescribes a specific cure for a person with difficulties in combating his temptations. That cure is immersing oneself in spiritual growth.

The reader may object that reincarnation is not a mainstream Jewish concept. In fact, although it has received its greatest elaboration among Kabbalists and their Hasidic successors, the two greatest "mainstream" rabbis of the 20th century both subscribed to the concept of "recycling of souls." Above we quoted from Rabbi I.M. Kagan. Here I want to mention that Rabbi A.I. Karelitz, referred to as "The Hazon Ish," (meaning "a seer of a man") used to stand up in respect when a retarded person would enter the room. He explained this strange behavior in terms of reincarnation.

Rabbi Karelitz pointed out that sometimes a great and holy person will commit one small sin. Even that small sin needs to be rectified, but in the process of coming into a new body in this world, many other sins may be committed. How is it possible for an elevated soul to enter this world and fix the one small sin without becoming encumbered with additional sins? If a soul is born into a mentally "retarded" body, he or she is considered exempt from the performance of the commandments, which are ostensibly beyond his or her capacity. Such

---

[154]   Talmud, Kiddushin 30b

a person cannot sin, because he or she is not obligated by the commandments. However, he or she can do that one positive act which will rectify the sin from the previous lifetime. Therefore, Rabbi Karelitz assumed that all retarded people were lofty souls, deserving of great honor.

Another reason why people suffer is to have a positive effect on other people, who, through caring for the afflicted person, will develop their own traits of kindness, patience, altruism, etc. Albert Einstein said, "Adversity introduces a man to himself." Not only does a person's adversity introduce the person to him/herself, but also that adversity may introduce other human beings to themselves.

As the father of a fourteen-year old girl who, after a massive prayer and good deeds campaign, succumbed to leukemia wrote:

My daughter had a very difficult path in life, but she fulfilled her task. She became part of so many different people's lives—hundreds, maybe thousands—most who never knew her. She elevated and inspired them to greater God-consciousness. The Talmud says that the one who inspires others to do is even greater than the one who does themselves. Think about how much heartfelt prayer was said, how much charity was given, how many acts of kindness, and how much repentance she inspired. She accomplished in her fourteen years more than many people do in a lifetime.[155]

Kabbalah teaches that while we are a community of seemingly disparate human beings, we are in actuality derived from one colossal, mammoth splintered soul, the soul of primordial Adam. In the grand scheme of life, each of us is a micro facet of that enormous soul with a staggering responsibility to perfect humanity. Thus every person in humanity serves a distinct role in helping us attain perfection. So instead of an indigent pauper being viewed as a derelict or malefactor, the poor person should be viewed as someone who is giving us the opportunity to reach perfection. An ill or elderly person should not be viewed as a burden or strain, but again as someone who is giving other members of humanity the opportunity to near perfection. No person should feel that they must confront crisis or challenge alone, for it is not their personal battle but it is humanity's challenge to share in and grow from.

---

[155] Written by R. Asher Resnick about his daughter, Ruchama Rivka, of blessed memory. Published by www.Aish.com

As the following poem illustrates:

> On the street I saw a small girl cold and shivering in a thin dress,
> with little hope of a decent meal.
>
> I became angry and said to God:
> 'Why did you permit this?
>
> Why don't you do something about it?'
>
> For a while God said nothing.
> That night he replied quite suddenly:
> 'I certainly did something about it.
> —I made you.'"

The Storehouse of Souls

A cryptic statement in the Talmud declares: "The son of David (Messiah) will not arrive until all souls have been deposited from the *guf*." [156]

Guf refers, Kabbalistically, to the storehouse in heaven that contains all the souls that have to enter the world. The Talmud is teaching that until all souls find their way from heaven to earth, Messiah can't come. This is the reason why religious Jews believe in propagating as much as possible; every soul that is born brings the world one step closer to Messiah's coming.

Interestingly, *guf* in Hebrew literally means a physical body. So the Talmud can also be saying: "The son of David will not arrive until the souls that must be reincarnated in the physical body have finished their task."

According to this reading, in order to bring Messiah we must work on rectifying the souls inhabiting our present bodies. Otherwise, the soul will later have to migrate into another body, delaying the Messiah's arrival another generation.

---

[156] Talmud, Sanhedrin, 62a

With all this in mind, we can attempt to explain one of the greatest atrocities recorded in Jewish history. The Yom Kippur liturgy tells the horrific story of the Ten Martyrs. Ten holy rabbis of the Mishnaic period were brutally put to death to satisfy the anti-Semitic caprice of a Roman ruler.

The Roman ruler, in studying the Torah, came upon the law that if someone kidnaps a fellow Jew and then sells him, the kidnapper is liable to the death penalty. The ruler, ever so interested in scheming to harm the Jews, realized that this law could serve as a pretext to execute ten sages for a crime that had been committed more than sixteen centuries earlier.

Joseph's ten brothers had kidnapped him and sold him into slavery. The Roman sent for ten great sages who were renowned for their great holiness and analytical expertise. He commanded: "Judge the following case authentically, without any deceit or cunning: What is the law if a man is found to have kidnapped a member of his Jewish brethren, and he enslaved him and sold him?"

They answered him, "That kidnapper is to die." So he told them that they would be punished for their ancestors, who kidnapped and sold their brother Joseph. He commanded that they accept this judgment upon themselves, for since their forefathers' time there had been none like them.

The rabbis asked for three days to ascertain whether this was decreed from on High. Rabbi Yishmael the High Priest purified himself, uttered the Divine Name, and ascended to heaven. There he inquired whether the decree emanated from God. He learned that indeed it did.

Over a period of time, the ten rabbis were each executed in a cruel manner, one more barbaric than the next. To satisfy the Roman ruler's daughter, who wanted to preserve Rabbi Yishmael's unparalleled beauty, her father ordered that Rabbi Yishmael's flesh be flayed from his face. The daughter then stuffed the skin to preserve the rabbi's handsome features for her to gaze upon. The Romans tortured Rabbi Akiva by lacerating his flesh with sharp-toothed combs.

The celestial Angels cried out bitterly, "Is this the Torah and this its reward? The enemy insults Your great and awesome Name, and reviles and blasphemes against the words of the Torah."

A voice from heaven responded, "If I hear another sound, I will transform the universe to water. I will turn the earth to astonishing emptiness. This is a decree from My Presence; accept it, you who delight in the two-thousand-year-old law!"

This awful historical account raises several questions: Why, of all people, were these rabbis chosen to receive the punishment of Joseph's brothers? Weren't there greater Jews in the times of the Exodus or the First Temple? What does the Roman despot mean, "For since their forefathers' time, there have been none like them?"

Kabbalah teaches that these ten holy sages were actually reincarnations of Joseph's ten brothers. Joseph's brothers were all holy people who died without receiving atonement for their sin against Joseph. These holy men were reincarnated and eventually suffered their destined punishments. The Roman ruler's words, "For since their forefathers' time, there have been none like them," were literally true. Although there had been greater people, nobody but these ten sages were the ten brothers. Their punishment was righteous and fair.

The Kabbalists (particularly the Ari, R. Isaac Luria) declare that, if necessary, the soul is reincarnated many times to afford it the opportunity for *tikkun*. If after many times it still hasn't fixed itself, the soul may be reincarnated into an animal, and after many attempts even into an inanimate object. As the Sh'lah[157] posits in his opus *Torah Or*, quoting the famed Kabbalist R. Shlomo Alkabetz:

Those people who reincarnate but who have not repented after their third reincarnation . . . will no longer reincarnate as humans, but instead as beasts and animals, both kosher and non-kosher. The less serious judgment receives precedence. This is intimated by the verse in Job: "God does all these things with man two or three times" [i.e. in human form two or three times and afterwards as an animal or even an inanimate object].

---

[157]   R. Isaiah Hurwitz (1560-1630)

Twenty-Three

Sodom

Two people are standing on a ladder. One is standing on the top rung, the other on the bottom rung. Which fellow is higher on the ladder? The great Hassidic master, the Rebbe of Kotzk gave a surprising answer: The man standing on the bottom rung is higher than the man standing on the top rung, because the man on the top rung has nowhere else to go but down, whereas the man standing on the bottom rung has nowhere else to go but up.

The same is true for becoming a better human. A person who seems to be spiritually impoverished may be on a higher plane than a very advanced personage because spirituality is assessed only by how much one is moving forward. A person born with refined character traits who never works to improve himself is inferior to a person born with crass traits who has moved from minus 2 to minus 1.

Becoming a truly mature adult and a spiritual human being is not easy. Nobody is perfect. As Salvador Dali wrote in *The Diary of a Genius*, "Have no fear of perfection. You will never reach it."

Feeling that you will never be able to live by the ideals espoused in this book may discourage you from even trying to improve your spiritual level. That is the wrong attitude. While some people are more spiritual than others, no human being wholly lacks spirituality.

In the Biblical story of Abraham and Sodom,[158] God informs Abraham that He plans on destroying the city and its evil inhabitants. Abraham beseeches God to spare the city. He argues that there must be *some* righteous people in the city. God responds that there isn't even one righteous person in the entire city.

This story always troubled me. After all, why would a righteous person live in such a wicked and depraved society? What was Abraham fantasizing about? The answer may be that Abraham was conjecturing that there must be individuals who, despite all the seemingly insurmountable evil, tried to rise, even a bit, above the evil. Although they would not have stood out as shining examples of piety, their feeble efforts to rise above the evil surrounding them would have qualified them as righteous. A person's spiritual level is subjective. How a person behaves relative to his or her society and the challenges of that particular period of time determine his or her spiritual level.

The story of John Ash can teach us a lot about the worth of every human being. John, a high-profile corporate attorney, owned a mansion in an exclusive Long Island suburb, a villa in the Bahamas, a Mercedes, a Jaguar, and a yacht. He considered himself a very important personage.

One spring morning, John took a leisure walk in New York's Central Park. John's case involving the Securities Exchange Commission and a major client was weighing heavily on his mind. He became lost in thought and didn't realize that he had veered off from the walking lane into a dangerous trap. The butt of a revolver aroused him from his reverie.

John looked up to see a well-dressed man who looked like a corporate executive. With him was a man who gave the appearance of a vagabond. The executive had the one who looked like a vagabond in handcuffs. The executive spoke up. He told John that his hostage knew an incriminating secret that could damn him for life. He had to do away with his hostage if he was ever to live without fear. The executive

---

[158]   Genesis, 18:20-33

demanded that John kill the secret-bearer. If John refused to squeeze the revolver, the executive would kill John and find somebody else to kill his hostage. The executive's rationale was, worst-case scenario, police investigators could trace the executive to the murder of the vagabond because they had a blackmail-type connection, whereas no one could trace him to the random murder of John.

John was in a complex quandary. What should he do? He stole a glance at the hostage and quickly surmised that the fellow was probably a homeless vagrant. Why should he give up his life for somebody so worthless? John thought of himself as man of success, and figured that this other fellow was a failure and loser. John deduced that his life was more important than the vagrant's life. John Ash pulled the trigger.

The vagrant fell to the ground. The executive walked away. John fled the scene with little remorse. After all, it was crystal clear that he was a more worthy human being than the man that he killed.

According to the Talmud, what John did was patently wrong. The Talmud teaches that God doesn't measure a person's worth by money or possessions. The common statement that "X is worth five million dollars" is an anathema in Torah. Also, according to the Talmud, no human being is capable of measuring the value of another human life.

The reasoning behind this is simple. The human being is set apart from the rest of the animal kingdom by the way s/he responds to complex challenges. If one confronts a challenge head-on and responds in a positive fashion, then one grows into a better human being. Because we can't see into the deeper recesses of somebody else's heart and mind to determine how much s/he has grown or what s/he has overcome, we cannot possibly determine that person's worth.

It turns out in our story that John's now dead "low-life vagrant" was once a successful businessman who lost everything because he didn't want to get involved in scandalous business affairs that he accidentally discovered.

The Talmud teaches that there's no way possible to judge another person—to know the real value of another human being. There's no way possible to know what hurdles someone has overcome, or the nature and magnitude of the tests that confront someone. Yet this is the true measure of a person.

Hopefully you won't have to encounter such a test in Central Park. But what about people you engage with in the street, in the mall, at work, or even at home? You thought you knew who they were, but do you really know their worth according to the measures we've been discussing? Do you know the magnitude of the tests they have faced and passed? Perhaps you will now view them in a different light. If other human beings start becoming greater in your eyes, it means that you've conquered a challenge, and you yourself have become a greater human being.

✻ Epilogue ✻

The Ultimate

The da Vinci Code

Imagine a person living in the 13th century. If this fellow could propel himself five hundred years into the future, into the 18th century, he would look around and, aside for changes in fashion, find himself in his familiar world. Now, if a fellow living in 1839 propelled himself a mere one hundred years into the future, the world where he lands would be unrecognizable to him: steam engines, trains, automobiles, telegraphs, telephones, electricity—wonder after wonder would confound him. The world during that century became totally transformed. And the rate of change has only accelerated since then. What happened?

In the second chapter of the Zohar we read: "In the six hundredth year of the sixth millennium (the Hebrew year 5600), a great light will shine forth from the heavens, causing a transformation in the world."

Indeed, that year heralded a drastic change in the world. The Hebrew year 5600 corresponds to the Christian year 1839-1840. This was the start of the industrial revolution. From that time onwards, extraordinary advances were made in science and technology. This is what the Zohar was talking about.

Not that knowledge was absent in earlier times. As a matter of fact Leonardo da Vinci, the great Italian artist was also a gifted inventor. He created designs for making a car, an aircraft, and a helicopter, hundreds of years before these were produced in modern times. We also demonstrated in chapter 10, the unparalleled, futuristic knowledge of the rabbis of the Talmud. There is no question that the knowledge was there but the time, it seems, was not ripe.

The revolution we just mentioned is a definite prelude to the future Messianic time that the Torah predicts. It is the fulfillment of the Biblical prophecies concerning this epoch. Genetic engineering in agriculture is ushering in an existence that will bear food in an infinitesimal amount of time. Biotechnology, sequencing the human genome, adult stem cells, and cloning has fostered the ability to halt disease and prepare indigenous replacement organs that will guarantee longevity. Researchers are even grappling with thwarting apoptosis (cell suicide), thus conquering the natural aging process.

With fertility advances today, multiple births are a common occurrence. Transportation and technology are also making great strides in realization of prophecies that travel to Israel will be ever expeditious and efficient. This entire theory concurs with Maimonides' view that the messianic age will be dependent on the natural progression of science and technology and not something of a miraculous nature.

Morality and ethics will be at their zenith with the arrival of Messiah. In Messianic times, strife, enmity, and hatred will end. Peace will abound. The third Temple will be built.

King Messiah will usher in an epoch in which all people will recognize God as supreme and all will become loyal to Him. As the Prophet Zachariah states: "God will be King over the entire world. On that day He will be one and His Name will be one."[159] When will this amazing time arrive?

Ushering in the Age

According to the Torah, the Messianic age will arrive before the seventh millennia, which is the Jewish year 6000. Since we are currently

---

[159] Zachariah 14:9

in the Jewish calendar year of 5766, this means that anytime within the next 234 years we will usher in this era. How can this be accomplished?

Messiah can come in one of two ways:

1. Humanity will earn Messiah by following God's Law.
2. The plight of humanity will be so critical and desperate that the Messiah will have to come to salvage the world from utter doom.

According to the second scenario, the moral level of humanity will be so abased that a foreign nation will come to power and wake us up from our lethargy and slumber. According to many sources, this situation will eventually morph into a Third World War. This war, religious and nuclear in nature, will center on Jerusalem, and will be far worse than both World Wars combined.

According to the Torah, the foreign nation will be the Muslim Arabs, whom the Bible refers to as the Ishmaelites.[160]   In the year 2047, God promised Abraham that the Ishmaelites would become a dominant world power. The fulfillment of this prophecy commenced in the secular calendar year 622 (which is the Biblical year 4383), with the founding of Islam. In their Jihad wars, Islam almost became the dominant power in the world, as they attempted to conquer Western Europe, marching to Vienna. A staggering biblical prophecy reveals that in the End of Days the Arabs will regain world dominance. According to *National Geographic Magazine* (January, 2002), Islam is now the fastest growing religion on earth. One in every five human beings alive today is Muslim.

Oslo, 1993

Fixated with championing peace in the Middle East, President Bill Clinton compelled Israeli Prime Minister Yitzhak Rabin to make concessions to an implacable enemy. Concessions deemed unimaginable and absurdly dangerous. Clinton also imposed on Rabin to release scores of Arab terrorists from Israeli jails. Rabin balked at the idea but under intense American pressure he caved in. Clinton's next demand was preposterous. He ordered Rabin to release an infamous terrorist who had firebombed a bus of Israelis. Rabin was

---

[160]   Sources are only available in the original Hebrew: Pirkei D'Rebi Eliezer 36:32, Eitz Hadaas Tov chapter 124, Daniel 7:4 & 7:25 Malbim ibid.

flabbergasted by the demand. Although making peace with the Palestinians was a definite priority for the besieged prime minister, this order was crossing the line. Clinton was relentless; Rabin capitulated to the deal. The released terrorist was Mohammed Atta, native of Jordan and a naturalized American citizen.

That name should sound familiar. A callous terrorist, hailing from Egypt, with an identical name, decided to spend time in the same country that secured the other Mohammed Atta's release. Egyptian Mohammed Atta arrived in America. Ultimately, Mohammed Atta visited the Twin Towers. It was perhaps his first visit to those towers but the world's last. Mr. Atta was one of the masterminds of the attack that almost crippled America. On September 11, 2001, Atta commandeered a jetliner into the World Trade Center.

God's retribution is measure for measure. Perhaps it is no coincidence that the ringleader of 9/11 shared a name with a notorious terrorist that America exonerated. Our mistakes came back to haunt us.

In February 1993, five months after the commencement of the Oslo Peace process, the World Trade Center was attacked for the first time. Tragically five people were killed but it could have been much worse. Subsequent to their first attempt at destroying the World Trade Center, Islamic fundamentalists planned to explode the bridges, tunnels, and train systems of New York City. The subway attacks of Madrid and London would have paled in comparison. The terrorists had elaborate plans and perfected equipment to execute their plans. Miraculously their well-concocted scheme was foiled.

In 2001, with no weapons (just a few box-cutters), Islamic fundamentalists hijacked four American airliners. They succeeded in destroying two of the world's greatest towers, smashed into the Pentagon and attempted to destroy the White House. Our greatest bastions of security failed us. The Secret Service, CIA, FBI and Pentagon were vulnerable, bewildered and traumatized.

The 1993 attack on the World Trade Center was a wake up call. The foiled plot to blow up the N.Y.C. subways, bridges and tunnels was a wake up call. We did not listen. We did not wake up.

El-Said Nossair, the assassin of Meir Kahane, was also the architect of the first terrorist attack against the World Trade Center and the subsequent plan to blow up all the major transportation systems. Amazingly, the American court system acquitted Nossair for Kahane's murder, despite the fact that there were numerous eyewitnesses to the murder.

A court-mandated search of Nossair's New Jersey apartment revealed his handwritten diary, which called for "jihad against the enemies of Islam" by "destroying the structure of their civilized pillars, their high world buildings which they are proud of." His words are eerie, when compared to verses from the Torah.

The Torah section read in synagogues the world over on the Sabbath preceding 9/11 was from Deuteronomy, Chapter 28. There are prophetic verses mentioned there which, seem to be a portent to what was about to occur:

> God will carry against you a nation from afar from the end of the earth, as an eagle will swoop, a nation whose language you will not understand, a brazen nation that will not be respectful to the old nor gracious to the young . . . It will besiege you in all your cities, until the collapse of your high and fortified walls in which you trusted (prided yourselves in) throughout your land . . .

Does a "nation from afar" refer to Saudi Arabia and other Middle Eastern Nationals? Is "as an eagle will swoop" the Biblical language for modern-day jetliners? Can "the collapse of your high and fortified walls" be referring to the World Trade Center?

I will not be so presumptuous to claim that I fully understand the meaning of these verses. Why was it that the seat of world capitalism, the world's greatest towers –crumbled in, what seemed, the bat of an eyelash? Perhaps the message was that we Americans, the world's prototype and bastion for democracy and liberty, morphed into selfish worshippers of materialism. Our society became one where we judged ourselves, and others, based on physical characteristics, material possessions and acquisitions. We idolized hedonistic movie stars, sex icons, tycoons and athletes, instead of revering people with real values and virtues.

Many of us weren't transformed by the maelstrom of September 11. We didn't associate the event with a spiritual charge. Two years later, another wake up call came. The new wake up call was in the form of an indisputable message from heaven.

On Saturday, February 1, 2003, the space shuttle Columbia was blown to pieces minutes before re-entering Earth. A small heap of paper survived the fiery disintegration of space shuttle Columbia, a 38-mile fall to Earth, and two months of exposure to rain and sun in a Texas field. The paper has been painstakingly restored by forensic scientists, yielding the flight diary and notes of Israeli astronaut Ilan Ramon. We Americans became privy to a message that plummeted from the heavens. Ilan Ramon's diary entry was all about the Sabbath. That is fascinating because the Sabbath is about channeling ones resources towards spiritual growth, personal reflection, and family union. A message that America is in dire need of.

NASA discovered that the horrific Columbia explosion was due to a simple piece of foam getting stuck in the wrong location. A small piece of foam destroyed the most sophisticated piece of technology built in recent times. Doesn't that wake you up? Doesn't that cause you to stop and think?

Abraham Lincoln once observed:

> We have been the recipients of the choicest bounties of heaven. We have been preserved, these many years, in peace and prosperity. We have grown in numbers, wealth, and power, as no other nation has ever grown, but we have forgotten God. We have forgotten the gracious hand, which preserved us in peace, and multiplied and enriched and strengthened us; and we have vainly imagined, in the deceitfulness of our hearts, that all these blessings were produced by some superior wisdom and virtue of our own. Intoxicated with unbroken success, we have become too self-sufficient to feel the necessity of redeeming and preserving grace, too proud to pray to the God that made us.

Back to the Ancient

Isn't it a bit intriguing that we, the most advanced people on the face of the planet, are engaged in a war with a country that was the cradle of ancient civilization? Iraq is the country that saw the birth of Abraham and monotheism. It is the place that is described in the first account of Genesis and seemed to have served as the home of the Garden of Eden. The words *apocalypse, Armageddon, End Of Days, Jihad, temple mount, theology* are words so common in our parlance. The 21st century seems to resemble a time from eons ago. What is going on?

According to the Torah, in the End of Days, the Arabs will act subhuman, executing horrendous and unimaginable attacks upon people around the world. They will first team up with Christian nations (which the Bible refers to as "Edom"[161]) against the Jewish people, and later go out to war against the Christians. They will be all pervasive, enmeshed in every part of their enemies' lands. The Arabs, joined by an evil country from the North, will wield tremendous power and be ruled by super-wealthy princes. Eventually the various wars will morph into a world war centered on Jerusalem. During this precarious epoch in history, the nations of the world will also be subjected to severe natural disasters.

The Messianic Era will usher in the supremacy of Torah and the restoration, without conflict, of the land of Israel to the Jewish people. With the coming of Messiah, the oppressive Arab power and their partner from the North will dissipate into thin air.

I think that it is clear that the war against terrorism is a theological and ideological battle, a religious war that will develop into a full-fledged world war. What is the source of the conflict? Most politicians, media commentators, and laypeople pin Muslim wrath on the Israeli-Palestinian conflict. Interestingly, that conflict boils down to, amongst other things, ownership over Jerusalem. To allege that the tiny nation of Israel, about the size of the state of New Jersey, is responsible for the world's great upheavals is logically ludicrous. Yet, when looking through the prism of the Biblical prophecies, the centrality of the Jewish nation and ultimately Jerusalem is inevitable.

Our generation seems to be the generation of Messianic times. We have two choices: We can ignore all the signposts and prophecies in a binge of self-assertion and hope to survive the outcome of the war on

---

[161]   Ibn Ezra, Genesis, 27:40, Ezekiel 38:3 Malbim ibid, Abarbanel ibid.

terror, or we can change and improve our morality, thus sparing ourselves dire punishment.

Of course, the messianic age can also come about by a rectification of humanity's ways. Option one is always available. The power to choose it is in our hands.

Who Will He Be?

The Messiah will be a Jewish male from the lineage of King David. He will be a person of extraordinary personal character as well as an outstanding Torah scholar. He will be totally subservient to God's Torah. He will be a selfless and humble individual whose mission will be to bring others towards an awareness of their Creator. He will succeed in awakening the masses to penitence.

Although Messiah will directly descend from the royal line of David's dynasty, this is not to say that he must come from a pristine, untarnished background. Nobody should be written off as an unsuitable candidate to be the Messiah. David's own inception was fraught with scandal. He was the great-grandson of Boaz and Ruth. Ruth was a Moabite convert to Judaism. Ruth descended from an incestuous relationship between the Biblical character Lot and his daughter. Boaz descended from the questionable union of Judah and Tamar, who was disguised as a prostitute. All this is a lesson to teach us that a person should never be branded as incompetent for leadership because of familial, sociological, or economical circumstances. We may be taken by tremendous surprise when the identity of the Messiah is revealed.